REAL
SALVATION

R. A. TORREY

REAL SALVATION

WHITAKER
HOUSE

Publisher's note:
This book originated as a series of sermons by R. A. Torrey. Certain words and phrases have been printed in boldface type for emphasis by the author. Other words and phrases have been slightly revised and updated for readability. However, the content of his message remains unchanged.

Unless otherwise indicated, all Scripture quotations are taken from the King James Version of the Holy Bible. Scripture quotations marked (RV) are taken from the Revised Version of the Holy Bible.

REAL SALVATION

ISBN: 978-1-62911-155-1
eBook ISBN: 978-1-62911-156-8
Printed in the United States of America
© 2014 by Whitaker House

Whitaker House
1030 Hunt Valley Circle
New Kensington, PA 15068
www.whitakerhouse.com

Library of Congress Catalog-in-Publication Data

Torrey, R. A. (Reuben Archer), 1856–1928
 [Real salvation and whole-hearted service]
 Real salvation / by R.A. Torrey.
  pages cm
 Originally published under title: Real salvation and whole-hearted service. New York : Fleming H. Revell Company, 1905.
 Summary: "R. A. Torrey challenges readers to wrestle with age-old questions of faith, redemption, and salvation"— Provided by publisher.
 ISBN 978-1-62911-155-1 (alk. paper)
 1. Salvation. 2. Evangelistic work. I. Title.
 BT751.T6 2015
 234—dc23

                          2014046115

1 2 3 4 5 6 7 8 9 10 ℻ 20 19 18 17 16 15 14

CONTENTS

"WHERE ART THOU?"

"Where art thou?"
—Genesis 3:9

My subject is the first question that God ever asked of man. You will find that question in Genesis 3:9: *"Where art thou?"* God asked Adam the question. Adam had sinned, and on the evening of that awful day, the voice of God in its majesty was heard rolling down the avenues of the garden of Eden. Adam had often heard God's voice before, and the voice of God had been the sweetest music to Adam up until this day. Adam knew no greater joy than that of glad communion with his Creator and his heavenly Father. But now all was different, and as the voice of God was heard rolling through the garden, Adam was filled with fear and tried to hide himself. That is the history of every son of Adam from that day till this day. When sin enters our hearts and our lives, we seek to hide from God. Every sinner is trying to hide from the presence and the all-seeing eye of God. This accounts for a very large share of the skepticism, infidelity, agnosticism, and atheism of our day. It is sinful man trying to hide from a holy God.

Men will give you many reasons why they are skeptics, many reasons why they are infidels and agnostics and atheists; but in the great majority of cases, the real reason is this: Men hope, by denying the existence of God, to hide themselves from the discomfort of God's acknowledged presence. That also accounts for very much of the neglect of the Bible. People will tell you that they do not read their Bibles because they have so much else to read, that they do not read their Bibles because they are not interested in the Bible, and that it is a dull and stupid book to them; but the real cause of man's neglect of Bible study is this: The Bible brings God near to us as no other book does, and because men are uneasy in the conscious presence of God, they neglect the book that brings God near.

This also accounts for much of the absenteeism from the house of God and its services. People will give you many reasons why they do not attend church; they will tell you they cannot dress well enough to attend church, that they are too busy and too tired to attend church; they will tell you that the services of God's house are dull and uninteresting; but, in the great majority of cases, the reason why men and women, both old and young, habitually absent themselves from the services of God's house is because the house of God brings God near and makes them uncomfortable in sin. Their desire to hide from God, more or less distinct, leads them to stay away from the house of God.

But Adam did not succeed in hiding from God, and neither will you succeed. No man ever succeeded in hiding from God. God said to Adam, *"Where art thou?"* (Genesis 3:9). Then Adam had to come out from his hiding place, meet God face-to-face, and make a full declaration of all his sin. Sooner or later, no matter how carefully you hide yourself from God, you will have to come out from your hiding place, meet face-to-face with the all holy God, and make full declaration of just where you stand in His presence.

I believe that God is putting the question of Genesis 3:9 to every man and woman—to every Christian and to every non-Christian. *"Where art thou?"* Where do you stand in regard to spiritual and eternal things? Where do you stand in regard to God, in regard to heaven, in regard to righteousness, in regard to Christ, in regard to eternity? *"Where art thou?"*

Every wise man will be glad to face and answer that question. Every truly intelligent man desires to know just where he is. In business, every wise businessman desires to know just where he stands financially. In our country, at a certain time of the year, every careful businessman will take an inventory of his stock-in-trade, cast up his accounts, and find out precisely what are his credits and precisely what are his debits, and how much his assets exceed or fall below his liabilities. He wants to know just where he stands. As a result of his scrutiny, he may discover that he does not stand as well as he thought he did. He may find that he is in debt, when he hoped that his capital exceeded his liabilities. If that is true, he wants to know it, in order that he may conduct his business accordingly. Many a man has made shipwreck in business through an unwillingness to face the facts and find out just where he stands.

Years ago in America, I knew a very brilliant businessman, a man really gifted along certain lines of business enterprise. But his affairs got into a tangled condition. His wise business friends came to him and advised him to go through his books and find out just where he stood. They said to him, "If you are in a bad shape, we will help you out." But the man was too proud to take their advice; he was too proud to admit that his business was in a bad way, so he refused to look into it. He shut his teeth, set his face like a flint, and tried to plunge through. But instead of plunging through, he plunged into such utter financial ruin that, although he was, as I have said, an exceptionally brilliant man in some directions, he came to such a complete financial shipwreck that he never got on his feet again; and when he died, he did not have money enough to pay his funeral expenses, and I had to pay them out of my own pocket, simply because he was not willing to humble his pride and face facts.

It is just so with many of you. You are too proud to face the fact that you are morally and spiritually bankrupt, so you decide to shut your teeth, set your face like a flint, and plunge through. You will plunge into utter and eternal ruin.

Every man wants to know where he stands physically. He wants to know what the condition is of his lungs, heart, stomach, and nerves. He may be worse off than he thinks he is; he may think his heart is sound when his heart is defective. But, if that be the case, he wants to know it; because if he knows that his heart is defective, he will not subject it to the strain that he otherwise would. Many a man who might have been doing good work on earth today lies in a premature grave because he was not willing to find out his real condition and act accordingly.

Every man at sea wishes to know just where his vessel is—its exact latitude and its exact longitude. I remember an instance that happened while we were crossing the Atlantic Ocean some years ago. We had been sailing for days beneath clouds and through fogs and were unable to take an observation by the sun, so we continued on by dead reckoning. One night, I happened to be on deck, and suddenly there was a rift in the clouds just where the North Star appeared. Word was sent below to the commanding officer. The captain of the vessel hurried up on deck, and I remember how he fairly laid across the compass and how carefully he took an observation by the North Star, that we might know exactly where we were.

Likewise, we may be sailing across a perilous sea, toward an eternal port, and every truly intelligent person reading this book will desire to know just where he is—his exact spiritual longitude and his exact spiritual latitude.

How Shall We Consider This Great Question?

First of all, we should consider it seriously. It is not a question to trifle with. It is a singular fact that when men and women who are intelligent and sensible about everything else—who would not think of trifling with the great financial questions of the day or with great social problems—come to this great question of eternity, they will treat it as a joke.

One night in an American city, a little shoe shiner on the street was blacking my boots, and as he worked over my shoes, I put to him the question "My boy, are you saved?" The boy treated it as a joke. I was not surprised; that is all you would expect of a poor, illiterate, uneducated shoe shiner on the street. But, men and women, it is not what you would expect of thinking men and thinking women, that when you come to these great eternal problems of God—eternity, salvation, heaven, and hell—they should be treated as a joke. But, alas! They are treated as a joke by some men and women. Any man or woman who trifles with questions like these plays the part of a fool. I don't care what your culture is, what your social position is, what your reputation is for scholarship; I don't hesitate to affirm that unless you have faced, or will face, this great question of your spiritual condition with the profoundest earnestness and seriousness, you are playing the part of a fool.

We should consider this question honestly. There are many people in our day who are trying to deceive themselves, trying to deceive others, and trying to deceive God. Many men who know in their inmost hearts that they are wrong try to persuade themselves that they are right, try to persuade others that they are right, and try to persuade God that they are right.

Men and women, you cannot deceive God. It will do you no good to deceive anybody else, and it is consummate folly to deceive yourself. The biggest fool on earth is the man who fools himself. Be honest. If you are lost, own it up; if you are on the road to perdition, acknowledge it; if you are not a Christian, say so. If you are an enemy of God, face the facts. If you are a child of the devil, admit it. Be honest—honest with yourself, honest with your fellow men, and honest with God.

In the third place, we should consider the question thoroughly. There are many people who are honest enough and serious enough, as far as they go; but they don't go to the bottom of things. They are superficial. They give these tremendous questions a few moments' thought, and then their weak minds weary, and they say, "I guess I am all right; I will take my chance." You can't afford to guess on questions like these; we must have, not probability, but absolute certainty. It will not satisfy me to hope I am saved; I must know that I am saved. It will not satisfy me to hope I am a child of God; I must know that I am a child of God. It will not satisfy me to hope that I am bound for heaven; I must know that I am bound for heaven. Do not lay these questions down until you have gotten to the bottom of them and know with an absolute certainty just where you stand.

In the fourth place, you should prayerfully consider these questions. God tells us in His Word, and we know from experience, that the heart is deceitful above all things and desperately wicked. (See Jeremiah 17:9.) There is nothing that the human heart is as deceitful about as its moral and spiritual condition. Every man and woman is, by nature, very sharp-sighted to the faults of others and very blind to his or her own faults. What we need is to face this question in prayer. You will never know where you stand until God shows you. Not till we pray at least the substance of David's prayer in Psalm 139:23–24—*"Search me, O God, and know my heart: try me, and know my thoughts: and see if there be any wicked way in me"*—and God sheds the light of His Holy Spirit into our hearts and shows us how He sees us will we ever know ourselves as we really are.

The great Scotch poet Robert Burns, I think, never said a wiser thing than when he wrote:

> O wad some Power the giftie gie us
> To see oursels as ithers see us!
> It wad frae mony a blunder free us,
> An' foolish notion.[1]

But, friends, there is something better than to see ourselves as others see us, which is seeing ourselves as God sees us. Oh, let us not leave until we see ourselves in the light of God's presence, as God sees us, which will be in answer to definite and earnest prayer.

One morning in an American city, I met the pastor of a church I had formerly pastored. As we met, he said to me, "Brother Torrey, I had an awful experience this morning." I said, "What was it, Brother Norris?" He said, "You know Mrs. —," mentioning a member of the church of which he was now pastor, whom I remembered. He said, "You know she is dying. She sent for me to come and see her this morning. I hurried to her home. The moment I opened the door and entered the room, she cried from her bed, 'Oh, Brother Norris, I have been a professing Christian for forty years. I am now dying and have just found out in my dying hour that I was never saved at all.'" The horror of it! To be a professing Christian for forty years and never find out that you have never really been a Christian at all till your life's at an end. Better find it

1. Robert Burns, "To a Louse, on Seeing One on a Lady's Bonnet at Church," 1786.

out then than in eternity, but better find it out in the dawn of your professed Christian experience than right now.

I do not doubt that there are many men and women who have been professing Christians for years but who have never been saved. After we had left Liverpool, I read in a paper, edited by a clergyman in that city, a letter complaining about our meetings. In this letter, addressed to the public press, the writer said, "These men produced the impression that some of our church members are not saved." Well, that is the impression we tried to produce, for that is the truth of God. In the Church of England, and in the Nonconformist bodies, you will find many men and women who are unsaved.

Once more, we should scripturally consider this question, according to the Book. God has given to you and me only one safe chart and compass to guide us on our voyage through life toward eternity. That chart and compass is the Bible. If you steer your course according to this Book, you steer safely; if you steer your course according to your own feelings, according to the specula-tion of the petty philosopher or the theologian, according to any-thing but the clear declaration of the only Book of God, you steer your course to shipwreck. Any hope that is not founded on the clear, unmistakable teaching of God's Word is absolutely worth-less. Any hope founded on that Book is a sure hope; any hope that is not built upon that Book is not worth anything.

In one of my pastorates, a young married couple had entrusted to them a sweet little child by the heavenly Father for a brief period. Then God, in His infinite wisdom—and wisdom in this case that was not altogether inscrutable—took that little child home to Himself. Their hearts were deeply sorrowful, and in the hour of their pain, I went to call upon them and, taking advantage of their tenderness of heart, pointed them to that Savior with whom their child was safely at home. And they professed to accept that Savior.

After some days and weeks had passed, and the first keenness of the sorrow had gone, they began to drift back into the world again, and I called upon them to speak with them. Only the wife was at home. I began by talking about the little child, and how safe and happy it was in the arms of Jesus, to all of which, of course, she gladly assented. Then I turned it a little bit and said to her, "Do you expect to see your child again?" "Oh," she said, "certainly; I have not a doubt that I will see my child again." I said, "Why do you expect to see your child again?" She said, "Because the child is with Jesus, and I expect when I die, I shall go to be with Him, too." I said, "Do you think you are saved?" "Oh, yes," she said, "I think I am saved." I said, "Why do you think you are saved?" "Because I feel so," she said.

I said, "Do you think you have eternal life?" "Oh, yes," she said, "I think I have eternal life." I said, "Why do you think you have eternal life?" "Because," she said, "I feel so." I said, "Is that your only ground of hope?" She said, "That is all." I said, "Your hope is not worth anything." That seems cruel, doesn't it? But it was kind. I said, "Your hope is not worth anything. Can you put your finger upon anything in the sure Word of God that proves you have everlasting life?" "No," she said, "I cannot." "Well, then," I said, "your hope is absolutely worthless." Then she turned on me, which she had a perfect right to do. It is quite right to talk back to preachers—I believe in it—and she began to talk back, saying, "Do you expect to go to heaven when you die?" I said, "Yes, I know I shall." She said, "When you die, you expect to be with Christ?" "Yes," I said, "I know I shall." She said, "Do you think you have everlasting life?" "Yes," I said, "I know I have." She said, "Can you put your finger on anything in the Word of God that proves you have eternal life?" I said, "Yes, thank God—John 3:36: '*He that believeth on the Son hath everlasting life.*' Now," I said, "I know I believe on the Son of God, and on the sure ground of God's Word, I know I have everlasting life."

Can you put your finger upon anything in the Word of God that proves you are saved? If you can't, I advise you to find out if you are saved; if not, be saved right now. And if you are saved, find out something in God's Word that proves it.

One thing more before I close, and that is a few suggestions that will help you consider the question "Where art thou?" First of all, *Are you saved, or are you lost?* You are either one or the other. Unless you have been definitely saved by a definite acceptance of a definite Jesus, Jesus Christ, you are definitely lost. There are only two classes—lost sinners and saved sinners. To which class do you belong?

Second, *Are you on the road to heaven or the road to hell?* You are on one or the other. There are only two roads. The Lord Jesus tells us that there are two, and only two—the broad road that leads to destruction and the narrow road that leads to life everlasting. (See Matthew 7:13–14.) Which road are you on? Are you on the road that leads up to God and heaven and glory, or are you on the road that leads down to Satan and sin and shame and hell?

Some years ago, an English sailor came into a mission in New York City, and as he passed out of the mission not very much affected, a worker at the door put a little card into his hand. On this card were printed these words: "If I should die tonight, I would go to _____." The place was left blank, and underneath was written, "Please fill up and sign your name." The sailor, without even reading the card, put it in his pocket and went down to the steamer and put that card in the edge of his bunk. On the journey over, he was thrown from the rigging and broke his leg. They took him down to his berth, and as he lay there day after day, that card stared him in the face. He looked at it one day—"If I should die tonight, I would go to _____." "Well," he said, "if I filled that out honestly, I would have to write, 'hell.' If I should die tonight, I would go to hell. But," he said, "I won't fill it out that way," and, lying there in his berth, he took Jesus Christ and filled out the card. "If I should die tonight, I would go to heaven." He came on to England, went back to New York, walked into the mission, and handed in the card with his signed name.

Suppose you had such a card to fill out—"If I should die tonight, I would go to _____." What would it be?

Again, *Are you a child of God or a child of the devil?* We live in a day in which many superficial thinkers are telling us that all men are the children of God. That is not the teaching of the Bible, and it is not the teaching of Jesus Christ. Talking to certain Jews, Jesus Christ says distinctly in John 8:44, *"Ye are of your father the devil."* And we are told in 1 John 3:10, *"In this the children of God are manifest, and the children of the devil."* And we are told distinctly in John 1:12, *"As many as received him, to them gave he power to **become** the sons of God."* Children of God or children of the devil—every one of us is either one or the other. Which are you?

When I was speaking more than a year ago in the city of Ballarat, Australia, there was a long line of educated Chinamen in attendance who listened to the sermon. I was preaching on this same message. I came to the point I have come to now, and I thought to myself, *I guess I will leave that out; that may offend somebody without doing any good.* But, somehow or other, God would not let me leave it out, so I put it in, declaring the whole counsel of God. The next night when I gave out the invitation, among the people who came to the front was almost the entire line of educated Chinamen, and when they got up to give their testimony, one of them said, "The reason why I came tonight and took Christ was this: I was here last night and heard Dr. Torrey say that everyone was a child of God or a child of the devil. I knew I was not a child of God, and therefore I knew I must be a child of the devil. I made up my mind I would be a child of the devil no longer, and, therefore,

I have come forward tonight to take Jesus Christ." I hope some of you will have as much sense as that educated Chinaman.

Again, if you are a professing Christian, what kind of a Christian are you? *Are you a mere formal Christian, or are you a real Christian?* You know there are two kinds. Are you one of these men who calls himself a Christian—who goes to the house of God on the Sabbath, takes Communion on the Sabbath, and perhaps teaches a Bible class or a Sunday school class on the Sabbath—but, for the rest of the week, runs around after the bars and the casinos and the clubs and all the frivolity and foolishness of the world? Are you one of these Christians who try to hold on to Jesus Christ with the one hand and to the world with the other? Or are you a real Christian who has renounced the world with your whole heart and given yourself to Jesus Christ with all your heart, a Christian who can sing "I surrender all" and mean it? "Where art thou?" What kind of a Christian are you?

Once more, *Are you for Christ, or are you against Him?* You know you are either one or the other, for He says so. We read Jesus' words: *"He that is not with me is against me"* (Matthew 12:30). Everyone reading this is either wholeheartedly, confessedly, and openly with Jesus or else is against Jesus. Which are you? For Christ or against Him?

In my first pastorate, year after year, for a series of years, there came an outpouring of God's Spirit. In the second or third of these gracious outpourings, a great many of the leading businessmen of the place were converted. It was a small place, but one of the leading businessmen would not take a stand. He was one of the most exemplary men in the community. Most amiable, attractive, upright, a constant attendant at church, a member of my Bible class, and a member of my choir; but he was one of those men who wanted to please both sides. He was identified with friends in business, in the Masonic lodge, and elsewhere who were not out-and-out Christians, and he was afraid that he would estrange them if he came out honestly for Christ. So the weeks passed by. One Sabbath morning in the Bible school, after the morning service, he was walking out of my Bible class on the choir platform and passed by the superintendent of the Sunday school, who was an intimate friend. They had been in the Civil War together. As he passed by, his friend turned to him and said, "George?" "Well, what is it, Porter?" said the other, calling him by his first name. He said, "George, when are you going to take a stand?" George said, "Ring the bell." Promptly the superintendent stepped up to the bell and rang it, and the congregation going out of the building turned round in surprise, wondering what was going to happen. George stepped to the front of the platform. It was a community where everybody knew everybody else by his first name, and everybody was very curious. Then he said, "Friends, I have heard it said time and time again during these meetings that a man must either be for Jesus Christ or against Him. I want you all to know that from this time on, Em [his wife] and I are for Christ." He decided for the whole family, and he did, in fact, for he stood before the platform to receive the right hand of fellowship into the church with his wife, father-in-law, brother-in-law, and sister-in law—every member of the family that was not already in the fold.

Men and women, there are many of you whose sympathies for years have been with the church of Jesus Christ, but you have never been man enough or woman enough to take an open stand. Take it today. Say, "As for me and my house, we are for Christ." (See Joshua 24:15.) Where art thou? Ask yourself the question.

There is one thing that makes it exceedingly important why you should face this question, and that is the fact that where you are right now will in all likelihood determine where you shall spend eternity.

A story is told of Dr. Forbes Winslow, an elder and an eminent pathologist in diseases of the mind. A young French nobleman came to London bringing letters of introduction from leading Frenchmen, including one from Napoleon III, who was emperor at that time, introducing him to Dr. Forbes Winslow and soliciting Forbes Winslow's best offices for the young man. He presented his letters, and Dr. Winslow said, "What is your trouble?" He said, "Dr. Winslow, I cannot sleep; I have not had a good night's sleep for two years, and unless something is done for me, I shall go insane." Dr. Winslow said, "Why can't you sleep?" "Well," said the young man, "I can't tell you." Dr. Winslow said, "Have you lost any money?" "No," he said, "I have not lost money." "Have you lost friends?" "No, I have not lost friends recently." "Have you suffered in honor or reputation?" "Not that I know of." "Well, then," said the doctor, "why can't you sleep?" The young man said, "I would rather not tell you." "Well," said Dr. Winslow, "if you don't tell me, I can't help you." "Well," he said, "if I must tell you, I will. I am an infidel. My father was an infidel before me, and yet, in spite of the fact that I am an infidel, and that my father was an infidel, every night when I lie down to sleep, I am confronted with the question, 'Eternity—where shall I spend it?' All night, that question rings in my ears: 'Eternity—where shall I spend it?' If I succeed in getting off to slumber, my dreams are worse than my waking hours, and I start from my sleep again." Dr. Winslow said, "I can't do anything for you." "What!" said the young Frenchman. "Have I come all the way over here from Paris for you to treat me for you to dash my hopes to the ground? Do you mean to tell me that my case is hopeless?" Dr. Winslow repeated, "I can do nothing for you, but I can tell you a Physician who can," and he walked across his study, took up his Bible from the center of the table, opened it to Isaiah 53:5–6, and began to read:

> *He was wounded for our transgressions, he was bruised for*
> *our iniquities: the chastisement of our peace was upon him;*

and with his stripes we are healed. All we like sheep have gone astray; we have turned every one to his own way; and the LORD *hath laid on him the iniquity of us all.*

And then, looking at the Frenchman, he said, "That is the only Physician in the world that can help you." There was a curl of scorn upon the Frenchman's lip. He said, "Dr. Winslow, do you mean to tell me that you, an eminent scientist, believe in that worn-out superstition of the Bible and Christianity?" "Yes," said Dr. Winslow, "I believe in the Bible, I believe in Jesus Christ; and believing in the Bible and believing in Jesus Christ has saved me from what you are today." The young fellow stopped and thought, and then he said, "Dr. Winslow, if I am an honest man, I ought at least to be willing to consider it, ought I not?" "Yes, sir." "Well," he said, "will you explain it to me?" And the eminent physician became a physician of souls. He sat down with his open Bible and, for several consecutive days, showed the young Frenchman the way of life. He saw Christ as his divine, atoning Savior, put his trust in Him, and went back to Paris in rest of mind to sleep at night. He had solved the great question of eternity and where he should spend it, for he would spend it with Christ in glory.

Men and women: *Eternity—where will you spend it?* Where you will spend eternity will very likely depend upon where you are right now.

2

THE APPALLING SIN
OF UNBELIEF

*"He that believeth on him is not condemned: but he that
believeth not is condemned already, because he hath not
believed in the name of the only begotten Son of God."*
—John 3:18

The failure to put faith in Jesus Christ is not a mere misfortune,
it is a sin—a grievous, appalling, damning sin. *"He that believeth on
him is not condemned: but he that believeth not is condemned already,
because he hath not believed in the name of the only begotten Son of
God."* Men will tell you very lightly and laughingly, "I do not believe
in Jesus Christ." Indeed, men will tell you, "I do not believe in Jesus
Christ," with an airy toss of the head, as if it were something of
which they were quite proud. Few men are so foolish and so blind,
or so utterly depraved, as to tell you laughingly or proudly, "I am a

murderer" or "I am an adulterer" or "I am a habitual liar," yet none of these is a sadder or darker confession than "I am an unbeliever in Jesus Christ."

Believing or not believing in Jesus Christ is largely a matter of the will, not altogether or largely a matter of intellectual conviction. There are those who imagine that whether one believes or does not believe in Jesus Christ is wholly a matter of intellectual conviction. The one who thinks so is a very superficial thinker. There are very few people who have not sufficient evidence that Jesus is the Son of God and the Savior of those who really believe in Him, if they were only willing to yield themselves to the evidence. The will plays a very large part in what a man believes politically, and the will plays a still larger part in believing in Jesus Christ. The men and women who believe in Jesus Christ believe in Him because they will to yield to the truth and to believe in Him who is so clearly and so abundantly proven to be God's Son. Those who do not believe in Jesus Christ do not believe in Him because they, for the love of sin, or for some other reason, will not yield to the truth and accept Him as Savior and Lord, who is so abundantly proven to be the Son of God.

Most of you who do not believe in Jesus Christ know that this is true of yourselves. You know that your refusal to accept Jesus Christ is not because you have grave reasons for believing that Jesus Christ is not what He claims to be. You know it is because you do not want to accept Him and surrender your life to Him and confess Him. Now, this is a great sin—a greater sin than any sins you can commit against any fellow man, either by lying to him, or stealing from him, or killing him; it is a greater sin than falsehood, theft, or murder. If you will give me your honest attention, I will prove to you that this is so. Now, don't try to get away from the truth. If you do, you will do it to your own eternal ruin. If I am right in this matter, and if the Bible is right, it is of infinite importance that you know it. So, listen carefully and candidly.

1. Unbelief in Jesus Christ is an appalling sin because of who Jesus Christ is and because of the dignity of His person. Jesus Christ is the Son of God, the only begotten Son of God. He is the Son of God in a sense that no other person is the son of God. He is the brilliance of His Father's glory and the express image of His person. (See Hebrews 1:3 RV.) In Him dwells all the fullness of the Godhead in a bodily form. (See Colossians 2:9.) He is the One of whom God the Father said, *"Let all the angels of God worship him"* (Hebrews 1:6). The Father says that all men should honor the Son even as they honor the Father. (See John 5:23.) A dignity attaches to the person of Jesus Christ that attaches to no angel or archangel, to none of the principalities or powers in the heavenly places. His is the name that is above every name; and at the name of Jesus, every knee should bow and every tongue confess that He is Lord. (See Philippians 2:10–11.)

An injury done to Jesus Christ is then a sin of vastly greater magnitude than a sin done to man. A horse, a cow, or a mule has rights; but the rights of a horse, cow, or mule are of very inconsiderable moment when compared to the rights of a man. The law recognizes the rights of a mule, but the willful killing of a mule is not regarded to be as serious as the willful putting out of a man's eye. But the rights of a man, even one of the purest, noblest, and greatest of men, pale into utter insignificance before the rights of that infinite Being whom we call God, and His infinite Son Jesus Christ, just as the rights of a horse or cow or mule or earthworm pale in comparison before the rights of man.

To realize the enormity of a sin committed against Jesus Christ, we must strive to get some adequate conception of the dignity and majesty of His person. When we do, we then see that to rob this infinitely glorious Person by our unbelief of that honor is a sin in comparison with which the rankest injustice or enormity committed against man is as nothing. What was it that struck conviction to the hearts of three thousand men on the day of Pentecost and made them cry out in agony, *"Men and brethren, what shall we do?"* (Acts 2:37). It was this—Peter, filled with the Spirit, told them who Jesus was. He said, *"Therefore let all the house of Israel know assuredly, that God hath made that same Jesus, whom ye have crucified, both Lord and Christ"* (Acts 2:36). Their eyes were opened at last to see the glory, the dignity, the majesty of the person of Him whom they had so outrageously wronged. All the sins of their lifetime were instantly seen to be nothing in comparison with this sin.

And if you will permit God to open your eyes to see who Jesus is, to see the infinite dignity, glory, and majesty of His divine person, you will see that every conceivable wrong done to any mere man is nothing in comparison to the wrong done to this majestic Person. You may refuse to let God open your eyes to the infinite glory of Jesus; you may say you don't see that He is essentially greater than other men or that His rights are more sacred than those of Longfellow or Lincoln or Washington or my next-door neighbor; but the day will come when you will have to see. The day will come when the full glory of Jesus will be unveiled to the whole universe; and if you will not repent now and receive pardon for your awful sin of unbelief in this glorious Son of God, you will be overwhelmed with eternal shame on that day. You will cry for the rocks and the hills to fall upon you and hide you from the wrath of Him who sits upon the throne of the universe—the wrath of the Lamb. You will wish to rush out from the presence of that ineffable glory even into eternal darkness if it shall only be away from the presence of Him whom you have so grievously wronged. On and on and on you would wish to flee; away, away, away, eternally away from the outraged Son of God.

One night, God gave me such a vision of the glory of Jesus Christ that I saw the appalling nature of sin against Him, this infinitely glorious One. Men and women, you may not have had such a vision; nor do you need to have it, for you know what God's own testimony regarding Jesus is. That testimony is in His Book. In the light of that testimony, you may know, if you will, that the most grievous wrong against man—theft, adultery, murder—is as nothing. It is for this reason that our text says, "*He that believeth on him is not condemned: but he that believeth not is condemned already, because he hath not believed in the name of the only begotten Son of God*" (John 3:18).

2. In the second place, unbelief in Jesus Christ is an appalling sin, not only because of the dignity of Christ's person, but also because faith is the supreme thing which is His due. Jesus is worthy of many things. He is worthy of our admiration, He is worthy of our attention, He is worthy of our obedience, He is worthy of our service, He is worthy of our testimony, He is worthy of our love— all these things are His due. Not to give Him these things is to rob Him of His due, to rob a Being of infinite importance of His due. But, first of all, underlying all else, above all else, Jesus Christ is worthy of faith; man's confidence is due Jesus Christ. He is infinitely worthy of the surrender of our intellects, feelings, and wills. It is due to Him that you go to Him and say, "Lord Jesus, Thou infinite Son of God, I surrender to Thee my mind's utter faith, the utter confidence of my heart and of my will." He is worthy of that, for it is His due, His first great due. If you refuse to do that—and many of you have refused to do it, week after week, month after month, and year after year—you have robbed Jesus Christ. You have robbed this glorious, divine Person of His first and greatest right, robbed a divine Person of His supreme due. So it is written in our text, "*He that believeth on him is not condemned: but he that believeth not is condemned already, because he hath not believed in the name of the only begotten Son of God.*"

3. In the third place, unbelief in Jesus Christ is an appalling sin because Jesus Christ is the incarnation of all the infinite moral perfections of God's own being. *"God is light, and in him is no darkness at all"* (1 John 1:5). This infinite, absolute light which God is, this infinite holiness and love and truth, is incarnate in Jesus Christ; and the refusal to accept Him is the refusal of light, as well as a choice of darkness. It is the clearest possible proof that the one who rejects Him loves darkness rather than light. Nothing more clearly proves what a man is at heart than what he chooses and what he rejects. A man who chooses foul books, foul pictures, and foul friends is a foul man, whatever his pretensions may be. A man who rejects what is good, pure, and true is bad, impure, and false. To reject Christ is to reject the infinite light of God, and the decision reveals a heart that is so corrupt that it loves darkness rather than light. So it is written in this text, *"He that believeth on him is not condemned: but he that believeth not is condemned already, because he hath not believed in the name of the only begotten Son of God. And this is the condemnation, that light is come into the world, and men loved darkness rather than light, because their deeds were evil"* (John 3:18–19). Unbelief in Jesus Christ is indeed an appalling sin.

4. In the fourth place, unbelief in Jesus Christ is an appalling sin because it is trampling underfoot the infinite love and mercy of God. Jesus Christ is the supreme expression of God's love and mercy to sinners. John 3:16 says, *"For God so loved the world, that he gave his only begotten Son, that whosoever believeth in him should not perish, but have everlasting life."* We have all broken God's holy laws and thus brought the wrath of the Holy One upon ourselves, but God still loves us and, instead of banishing us forever from His presence into the outer darkness, where there is only agony and despair, has provided a way of salvation for us. He provided that way at infinite cost to Himself. His saving love had no limit, and it stopped at no sacrifice. He gave His best, His only begotten Son, to redeem us. All that we need to do to be saved is to believe

in His Son, to put our trust in the pardoning mercy and love of God thus revealed.

But instead of believing, and thus obtaining eternal life, what are many of you doing? You are not believing and are rejecting this love and its provision. You are despising and trampling underfoot the salvation which God has so dearly purchased and offered to you. You are scorning and insulting infinite love and mercy. That is what unbelief in Jesus Christ is—scorn and contempt and insult to infinite, pardoning love. All men and women, young and old, who do not render the faith of their whole being to Jesus Christ, who do not receive Him as the Son of God and as their Lord and Savior, are guilty of scorning and insulting the infinite, pardoning love of God. Some of you go even beyond that: You try to make yourselves believe that Jesus is not the Son of God; you try to make yourselves believe that there is no need of an atonement; you laugh at the sacrifice the loving Father has made in order that you, His guilty, hell-deserving subjects, might be saved. Yes, there are men and women who do this. There are thousands in this country who do it. One sometimes almost wonders why the outraged love of God does not turn to blazing wrath, and why God does not blast the world of Christ-rejecting men with the breath of His mouth. Unbelief in Jesus Christ is an appalling sin because it is scorn and contempt for infinite love.

There are other reasons why unbelief in Jesus Christ is an appalling sin, but I will give you only four tremendous reasons, because they are enough. Unbelief in Jesus is appalling, first, because of the infinite dignity of His person; second, because faith in Him is His supreme due, and not to give it is to rob this divine Person; third, because Jesus Christ is the incarnation of all the infinite moral perfection of God's own being; and, fourth, because it is trampling underfoot the infinite love and mercy of God.

Men and women, it is as clear as day that unbelief in Jesus Christ is an appalling sin. Theft is a gross sin, adultery is worse, murder is shocking; but when our eyes are opened, we see that all these are as nothing to the violation of the dignity and majesty of the person of Jesus Christ, the only begotten Son of God, by our unbelief. How God must despise the sin of unbelief! How the holy angels in heaven must despise the sin of unbelief! How all holy men and women must despise the sin of unbelief! And of this awful, appalling sin, many of you whom I address are guilty. Not only the gross infidel and the refined skeptic are guilty of this sin, but everyone who holds back from giving to Jesus the whole-hearted surrender of his whole self, mind, affections, and will.

All who fail to gladly welcome Him as Savior and Lord are guilty of this appalling sin. Do not some of you cry out, as did the three thousand at Pentecost, *"What shall we do?"* (Acts 2:37). Then it is because of the hardness of your heart. Soften your heart of stone; publicly confess your awful sin; forsake it right now. Don't rest another day under such awful guilt. We see why it is that unbelief leads to eternal doom. We see why it is that no matter how many good things a man may do, if he refuses to believe in Jesus Christ, he must forever perish. Men and women, give up your awful unbelief in Jesus Christ and accept Him today.

3

HELL: ITS CERTAINTY, WHAT SORT OF PLACE IT IS, AND HOW TO ESCAPE IT

"And if thy right eye causeth thee to stumble, pluck it out, and cast it from thee: for it is profitable for thee that one of thy members should perish, and not thy whole body be cast into hell."
—Matthew 5:29 (RV)

My subject in this chapter is hell: its certainty, what sort of place it is, and how to escape it. If I were to choose my own subject to write upon, I certainly would never choose this. I always speak and write upon it with reluctance and pain. It is an awful subject, but a minister of God has no right to choose his own subjects. He must go to God for them, and I am confident that God wishes me to write upon this awful subject.

I wish that I could believe that there was no hell—that is, I wish that I could believe that all men would come to repentance and accept Christ, and that hell should therefore be unnecessary. Of course, if men will persist in sin and persist in the rejection of Christ, God's glorious Son, I cannot but recognize that it is right that there should be a hell, and that that hell should continue as long as men persist in their sin and their rejection of Christ. If men will choose sin, it is for the good of the universe and the glory of God that there should be a hell to confine them in; but I wish with all my heart that all men would repent and thus render hell unnecessary, as far as the human race is concerned. But I do not wish to believe it if it is not true. I would rather believe and write about unpleasant truth than to believe and write about pleasant error. And, as awful as the thought is, I have been driven to the conclusion that there is a hell. I once honestly believed and taught that all men, and even the devil, would ultimately come to repentance, and that hell would thus cease to be. But I came to a place where I could not honestly reconcile this position with the teaching of Christ and the apostles. I was driven to this alternative—that I must either give up my Bible or give up my "eternal hope." I could not give up the Bible. I had become thoroughly convinced that the Bible was, beyond a doubt, the very Word of God. I could not in honesty twist and distort the Scriptures to make them agree with what I wanted to believe. As an honest man, I was left with only one thing to do, and that was to give up my opinion that all men would ultimately come to repentance and be saved.

I know perfectly well that if a man stands squarely upon the teaching of Christ and the apostles and declares it without fear, he will be called "narrow," "harsh," and "cruel." But, as to being narrow, I have no desire to be any broader than Jesus Christ was; as to being cruel, is it cruel to tell men the truth? Is it not the kindest thing that one can do to declare the whole counsel of God and to point out to men the full measure of their danger?

Suppose that I were walking down a railway track, knowing that, far behind me, there was a train coming on, loaded with happy excursionists—men, women, and children full of joy and glee. I come to a place where I had supposed that there was a bridge across the chasm, but, to my horror, I find that the bridge is down. I say to myself, "I must go back at once as far as possible up the track and stop that oncoming train." I hurry back and put forth my utmost effort to stop the train. I break in upon the people with the awful announcement that the bridge is down and that they are in peril of a frightful disaster. I spoil the merriment of the evening, banishing the bright thoughts from their minds and bringing instead horrid thoughts of imminent disaster. Would that be cruel? Would it not be the kindest thing that I could do?

Suppose, on the other hand, when I had found the bridge down, I had said, "These people are so happy, I cannot bear to disturb their night's lightheartedness and gaiety; that would be too cruel. I will sit down here and wait till the train comes." So, I sit down while the train comes rushing on and leaps unwarned into that awful abyss, and soon there arise despairing shrieks and groans of the wounded and mangled people as they crawl out from among the corpses of the dead. Would that be kind? No. Is it not the cruelest thing that I could do? In my country—and, I suppose, in yours—if I had acted that way, I would be arrested for manslaughter.

Friends, I have been down the track. I had supposed that there was a bridge across the chasm. I have found that the bridge is down. Perhaps many of you who are now full of gaiety and joy are rushing on, unwarned of the awful fate that awaits you. I have come back up the track to warn you. I may banish, for the time being, your joyfulness and merriment; but, by God's grace, I will save you from the awful doom. Is that cruel? Is it not the kindest thing that I can do? I would much rather be called cruel for being kind than be called kind for being cruel. The cruelest man on earth is the man who believes the stern things we are told in the Word of God about the future penalties of sin but keeps back from declaring them because they are unpopular.

I shall not give you my own speculations about the future destiny of the impenitent. My speculations would be worth as much as those of other men, and no more. That is, they would be worth practically nothing at all. Man's speculations on such a subject are absolutely valueless. God knows, we don't; but God has been pleased to tell us much of what He knows about it. Let us listen to Him. One ounce of God's revelation about the future is worth a hundred tons of man's speculation. One hears on every side in these days, "I think such and such about the future life." What difference does it make what you think? The question is, What does God say?

My text here is Matthew 5:29 (rv): *"And if thy right eye causeth thee to stumble, pluck it out, and cast it from thee: for it is profitable for thee that one of thy members should perish, and not thy whole body be cast into hell."* You will notice that it is from Jesus' Sermon on the Mount. I did this for two reasons—first of all, because it exactly suits my purpose; second, because a great many men say in our day that though they do not believe in the whole Bible, they do believe in the Sermon on the Mount. Well, I have taken my text from that part of the Bible that you all say you believe.

And you will notice that I have taken it from the Revised Version. I have done that for two reasons: first of all, because the Revised Version, in this instance, is a more accurate translation than the Authorized Version; and, second, because a great many men say that the Revised Version has done away with hell. Well, there seems to be plenty of it left in the text. "But," you say, "that text is highly figurative." Very well—let it go at that. It at least means this much, that almost anything is better than going to hell, and that is my chief proposition. Almost anything is better than going to hell.

What I have to say will come under three heads: first, the certainty of hell; second, the character of hell; and, third, how to escape hell.

The Certainty of Hell

It is absolutely certain that there is a hell. There are people who will tell you that all the scholarly ministers and clergymen have given up belief in the orthodox hell. That simply is not so. That kind of argument is a favorite with men who know that they have a weak case, and they try to bolster up a weak case by strong assertion. It is true beyond a doubt that some scholarly ministers have given up belief in the orthodox hell, but they never gave it up for reasons of Greek or New Testament scholarship. They gave it up for purely sentimental and speculative reasons. No man can go to the New Testament to find out what it really teaches and not find the reality of hell, unless he does it to see how he can twist it into conformity with the speculations he wishes to believe.

But suppose it were true. Suppose that every scholarly minister had given up belief in the orthodox hell—it would not prove anything; for everybody who is familiar with the history of the world and the history of the church knows that, time and time again, the scholars have all given up belief in doctrines that, after all, in the final outcome, proved to be true. There were no scholars in Noah's day except Noah who believed there would be a flood, but the flood came, just the same. There were no scholars in Lot's day except Lot who believed that God would destroy Sodom and Gomorrah, but He did. Jeremiah and one of his friends were the only leading men in all Jerusalem who believed in the coming destruction of Jerusalem under Nebuchadnezzar, but history outside the Bible, as well as history inside the Bible, tells us that it came true down to the very letter, though there was not a scholar who believed it. Every leading school of theological thought in the days of Jesus Christ—the Pharisees, the Sadducees, the Herodians, and the Essenes—scoffed at Jesus Christ's prediction about the coming judgment of God upon Jerusalem; but secular history tells us that, in spite of the dissent of all the scholars, it came true, just as Jesus Christ had predicted. In the days of Martin Luther and John Huss, there was not a university in the world or a leading scholar that had not given up faith in the doctrine of justification by faith; but Luther and Huss and their colleagues came and established a new university to stand for the truth of God. Today, we know that Martin Luther was right, and that every university of Germany, France, England, and Scotland was wrong. So, if it were true that every scholarly preacher on earth had given up belief in the doctrine of the orthodox hell, it would not prove anything.

Hell is certain. Why? First of all, because Jesus Christ says so, the apostles say so, and God says so. If you want the words of Jesus Christ, turn to Matthew 25:41:

> *Then shall he say also unto them on the left hand, Depart from me, ye cursed, into everlasting fire, prepared for the devil and his angels.*

If you want the words of Paul the Apostle, turn to 2 Thessalonians 1:7–9:

> *The Lord Jesus shall be revealed from heaven with his mighty angels, in flaming fire taking vengeance on them that know not God, and that obey not the gospel of our Lord Jesus Christ: who shall be punished with everlasting destruction from the presence of the Lord, and from the glory of his power.*

If you want the words of the apostle John, turn to Revelation 20:15:

Whosoever was not found written in the book of life was cast into the lake of fire.

If you want the words of the apostle Peter, turn to 2 Peter 2:4, 9:

God spared not the angels that sinned, but cast them down to hell, and delivered them into chains of darkness, to be reserved unto judgment;…the Lord knoweth how to deliver the godly out of temptations, and to reserve the unjust unto the day of judgment to be punished.

If you want the words of the apostle Jude, turn to Jude 14–15:

The Lord cometh with ten thousand of his saints, to execute judgment upon all, and to convince all that are ungodly among them of all their ungodly deeds which they have ungodly committed, and of all their hard speeches which ungodly sinners have spoken against him.

Again, if you want the words of Jesus Himself—after He had died, after He had gone down into the abode of the dead, after He had come up again, after He had ascended to the right hand of His Father—He certainly knows what He is talking about now, for He has been there, as you will find in Revelation 21:8:

The fearful, and unbelieving, and the abominable, and murderers, and whoremongers, and sorcerers, and idolaters, and all liars, shall have their part in the lake which burneth with fire and brimstone: which is the second death.

Hell is certain because Jesus Christ says so, the apostles say so, and God says so through them. The only things against it are the speculations of theologians and the dreams of poets.

The words of Christ have stood the test of eighteen centuries, and every time, they have proved true in the final outcome. No school of theological speculation has ever stood the test of eighteen years; and when I have Christ on one side and speculative theologians on the other, it doesn't take me long to decide which to believe.

In the second place, hell is certain because experience, observation, and common sense prove that there is a hell. One of the most certain facts of every man's experience is this—that where there is sin, there must be suffering. We all know that. The second certain fact of observation is that the longer a man continues in sin, the deeper he sinks down into the ruin, shame, agony, and despair that are the outcome of all sin. Gentlemen, there are hundreds and thousands of men and women in your city right now in a very practical hell, and the hell is getting worse every day. You may not know how to reconcile what these men and women suffer with the doctrine that God is love, but no intelligent man gives up patent facts because he cannot explain the philosophy of them; and this is a patent fact.

Now, if this process keeps going on—sinking ever deeper and deeper into ruin, shame, and despair—then, when the time of possible repentance has passed, and it must be passed some time, what is left but an everlasting hell? Again, the only things against it are the dreams of poets and the speculations of would-be philosophers. But the speculations of philosophers have proved an *ignis fatuus* from the very dawn of history; and when, on the one hand, I have the teaching of observation, experience, and common sense, and on the other hand, only the speculations of philosophers and the dreams of poets, it doesn't take me very long to decide which to believe.

But when, in addition to the teaching of observation, experience, and common sense, in its conflict with the speculations of cloistered theologians, we have the sure teaching of the Word of God, the case is settled. There is a hell. It is more certain that there is a hell than that, when you lie down to sleep tonight, you will wake again tomorrow morning. You probably will, but you may not; either way, it is absolutely certain that there is a hell. And the next time you buy a book—I care not how skillfully it is written—or go to hear a lecturer—I care not how eloquent—and pay a little bit of money, or a lot of money, to have some man prove to you by book or lecture that there is no hell, you are either paying a little bit of money or a lot of money to be made a fool of. There is a hell.

The Character of Hell

1. First of all, hell is a place of extreme bodily suffering. That is plain from the teaching of the New Testament. The commonest words to express the doom of the unrepentant are *death* and *destruction*, constantly recurring. What is meant by "death" and "destruction"? God has taken pains to define His terms. You will find His definition of destruction in Revelation 17:8, compared with Revelation 19:20 and Revelation 20:10. In Revelation 17:8, we are told that the beast goes into "*perdition.*" The word translated "perdition" is the same word that is translated "destruction" elsewhere, and it ought to be so translated here, or else it ought to be translated differently in the other passages. Now, if you can find where the beast goes, you have God's own definition of perdition, or destruction.

Turn to Revelation 19:20. You will read that the beast and the false prophet were cast into "*a lake of fire burning with brimstone.*" Turn to Revelation 20:10, and you are told that a thousand years after the beast and the false prophet have been thrown in there, the devil also is cast in at the end of the thousand years, and they shall be "*tormented day and night for ever and ever.*" By God's own definition, "perdition," or "destruction," is a place in a lake of torment forever and ever.

Now let us look at God's definition of death. You will find it in Revelation 21:8:

> *The fearful, and unbelieving, and the abominable, and murderers, and whoremongers, and sorcerers, and idolaters, and all liars, shall have their part in the lake which burneth with fire and brimstone: which is the second death.*

God's definition of "death" is a portion in "*a lake which burneth with fire and brimstone,*" just the same as His definition of "perdition." "Oh," somebody says, "that is all highly figurative." Very well, I don't care to contend against that at this moment; but, remember, God's figures stand for facts. When they come to something unwelcome in the Bible, some people will say it is figurative, and fancy that they have done away with it altogether. You have not done away with it by calling it figurative. What does the figure mean? God is no liar, and God's figures never overstate the facts. It means at least this much—bodily suffering of the most intense kind.

Remember furthermore that in the next life, we do not exist as disembodied spirits. All this theory so common today of the immortality of the soul independent of the body, where we float around as disembodied spirits, is Platonic philosophy and not New Testament teaching. According to the Bible, in the world to come, the redeemed spirit has a body—not this same body but still a body, a radically different body, the perfect counterpart of the redeemed spirit that inhabits it, and partaker with it in all its blessedness. On the other hand, the lost spirit has a body—not this same body but a body that is the perfect counterpart of the lost spirit that inhabits it, and partaker with it in all its misery. Why, even in the life that now is, inward spiritual sin causes outward bodily pain. How many men are suffering the most exquisite bodily suffering because of inward sin? I once went to a hospital where there were upward of twelve hundred people suffering the most awful bodily suffering, and the physician in charge told me that every one of the upward of twelve hundred were brought there by one specific sin. Friends, hell is the hospital of the incurables of the universe, where men exist in awful and perpetual pain.

2. But while there is physical pain, this is the least significant feature of hell. Hell is a place of memory and remorse. In the picture Christ has given us of the rich man in hell, Abraham said to the rich man, "*Remember*" (Luke 16:25). The rich man had not taken with him much that he had had on earth, but he had taken one thing—his memory. You men and women who go on in sin and spend eternity in hell won't take much with you that you own, but you will take one thing—your memory. You men will remember the women whose lives you blasted and ruined, and you women will remember the lives squandered in frivolity and fashion and foolishness, when you might have been living for God. You will remember the Christ whom you rejected and the opportunities for salvation that you despised.

There is no torment known to men like the torment of an accusing memory. I have seen in my office in Chicago strong men weeping like children. What was the matter? Memory. I have seen one of the strongest, brainiest men I have ever known throw himself upon the floor of my office and roll and sob and groan and wail. What was the matter? Memory. I have had men and women hurry up to me at the close of a service with pale cheeks, drawn lips, and haunted eyes, and beg a private conversation. What was the matter? Memory. You will take your memory with you; and the memory and the conscience that are not set at peace by the atoning blood of Christ and the pardoning grace of God in the life that now is, never will be. Hell is the place where men remember and suffer.

One day, Mr. Moody asked me to go out riding; and after we had ridden a little way, he drove into a cornfield, went out to the middle of the lot, and then said, "This is where it happened." I said, "This is where what happened?" He said, "Don't you remember, the last time I was in Chicago, I told you a certain story, and you said the next time you came to Northfield, you wanted me to show you just where it happened? This is where it happened."

What was the story? One day, when Mr. Moody was a mere lad, he was hoeing corn across a field with an elderly man. Suddenly, the man stopped hoeing and commenced hitting a stone with the hoe. Mr. Moody looked at him. Tears were rolling down the man's cheeks, and he said, "Dwight, when I was a lad like you, I left home to make a living for myself." His house was up on the hill; Mr. Moody pointed to it. The man continued, "As I came out of the front gate yonder, my mother handed me a Testament and said, 'My boy, "Seek ye first the kingdom of God, and his righteousness; and all these things shall be added unto you."'" He said, "I went to the next town. I went to church on the Sabbath. The minister got up to preach. He announced his text, Matthew 6:33, looked right down, pointed his finger at me, and said, 'Young man, "Seek ye first the kingdom of God, and his righteousness; and all these things shall be added unto you."'"

He said, "I went out of the church; I had an awful struggle! It seemed as if the minister were talking at me. I said, 'No; I will get fixed in life first, and then I will become a Christian.'"

Then he said, "I found no work there. I went to another town, and there I found employment. I went to church, as was my custom, Sunday after Sunday. After I had been going some Sundays, the minister stood up in the pulpit and announced his text, Matthew 6:33, 'Seek ye first the kingdom of God, and his righteousness; and all these things shall be added unto you.'"

And he said, "Dwight, he seemed to look right at me and point his finger right at me, and he said, 'Young man, "*Seek ye first the kingdom of God, and his righteousness; and all these things shall be added unto you.*"'"

He said, "I got up and went out of church. I went to the cemetery behind the church and sat down upon a tombstone. I had an awful fight, but at last I said, 'No, I will not become a Christian till I get settled in life.' And, Dwight, from that day to this day, the Spirit of God has left me, and I have never had the slightest inclination to be a Christian."

Mr. Moody said, "I did not understand it then. I was not a Christian myself. I went to Boston and was converted. Then I understood it. I wrote to my mother and asked her what had become of him, and she wrote, 'Dwight, he has gone insane, and they have taken him to the Brattleboro Insane Asylum.' I went home to Brattleboro and called on him there. He was in his cell, and as I went into his cell, he glared at me, pointed his finger at me, and said, 'Young man, "*Seek ye first the kingdom of God, and his righteousness,*"' and I could do nothing with him. I went back to Boston. After some time, I came home again. I said to my mother, 'Where is Mr. — now?' 'Oh!' she said, 'He is home, but he is a helpless imbecile.' I went up to his house. There he sat, rocking back and forth in a rocking chair, a white-haired man; and as I went into the room, he pointed his finger at me and said, 'Young man, "*Seek ye first the kingdom of God, and his righteousness.*"' Gone crazy with memory."

Men, hell is the madhouse of the universe, where men and women remember.

3. Again, hell is a place of insatiable and tormenting desire. You remember what Jesus tells us of the rich man in hell. The rich man said, "*Send Lazarus, that he may dip the tip of his finger in water, and cool my tongue; for I am tormented in this flame*" (Luke 16:24).

What is it a picture of? It is a picture of this, men: There is another thing you will carry into the next world with you. You will carry into the next world the desires that you build up here. Hell is the place where desire and passion exist in their highest potency, and where there is nothing to gratify them.

You men and women who are living in sin, living in worldliness, what are you doing? You are developing in your soul passions and desires, until they become regnant, for which there is no gratification in that world to which you are going. Happy is that man or woman who sets his or her affection on the things above in the life that now is, rather than cultivating desires and aspirations for which there is no satisfaction in the world to which we are going. Wretched indeed is that man or woman who cultivates ruling powers, passions, and desires for which there is no gratification in the world to which we are going.

4. In the fourth place, hell is a place of shame. Oh, the awful, heartbreaking agony of shame. When I was in New York, we had a cashier in a bank who was in a hurry to get rich, so he appropriated the funds of the bank and invested them, intending to pay them back. But his investment failed. For a long time, he kept the books so as to blind the bank examiner; but one day, when the bank examiner was going over them, he detected the embezzlement. He called in the cashier, who had to acknowledge his defalcation. He was arrested, tried, and sent to the state's prison. He had a beautiful wife and a lovely child, a sweet, angel-like little girl. Sometime after his arrest and imprisonment, the little child came home sobbing with a breaking heart. "Oh," she said, "Mother, I can never go back to that school again. Send for my books." "Oh, my darling," her mother responded, thinking it was some childish whim, "of course you will go back." "No," she said, "Mother, I can never go back. Send for my books." So she asked, "Darling, what is the matter?" Her daughter replied, "Another little girl said to

me today, 'Your father is a thief.'" Oh, the cruel stab! The mother saw that she could not go back to school. The wound was fatal. That fair blossom began to fade. A physician was called in, but it surpassed all the capacities of his art. The child faded and faded, until they laid her upon her bed, and the physician said, "Madam, I must tell you, this is a case in which I am powerless; the child's heart has given way with the agony of the wound. Your child must die." The mother went in and said to her dying child, "Darling, is there anything you would like to have me do for you?" "Oh," she said, "yes, Mother: Send for Father. Let him come home and lay his head down on the pillow beside mine, as he used to do." Ah! But that was just what could not be done. The father was behind iron bars. They sent to the governor of the state, and he said, "I have no power in the matter." They sent to the warden of the prison, and he said, "I have no power in the matter."

But hearts were so touched that they got together the judge and every member of the jury and the governor, wrote up a petition, and made arrangements whereby the father was suffered to come home under a deputy-warden. He reached his home late at night and entered his house. The physician was waiting. He said, "I think you had better go in tonight, for I am afraid your child will not live till morning." The father went to the door and opened it. The child looked quickly up. "Oh," she said, "I knew it was you, Father. I knew you would come. Father, come and lay your head beside mine upon the pillow, just as you used to do." And the strong man went and laid his head upon the pillow, and the child lovingly patted his cheek and died—killed by shame. Men and women, hell is the place of shame, where everybody is dishonored.

5. Hell is also a place of vile companionships. Do you want to know the society of hell? Read Revelation 21:8:

The fearful, and unbelieving, and the abominable, and mur-derers, and whoremongers, and sorcerers, and idolaters, and

*all liars, shall have their part in the lake which burneth with
fire and brimstone: which is the second death.*

That is the society of hell. "Oh," somebody says, "but many
who are brilliant and gifted are going there." It may be, men, but
listen: How long will it take the most gifted man or woman to sink
in such a world as that? Come to Chicago. I can go to the lowest
dives and pick you out men who were once physicians, lawyers,
congressmen, college professors, leading businessmen, and even
ministers of the gospel, who are now living with thugs, prostitutes,
and everything that is vile and bad. How did they get there? They
began to sink.

In 1864, when George B. McClellan was nominated on the
Democratic ticket for president of the United States, my father
was one of the delegates to the presidential convention in Chicago.
We then lived in New York. He took us children with him nearly
to the convention, left us in a quiet country town in Michigan, went
on to the convention, and then came back for us before we started
east. The train was filled with leading politicians. When we got to
Albany, we left the train and got on a steamboat in the Hudson
River. This steamboat was filled with the leading Democratic politicians, and we had a political meeting for hours that evening. Man
after man of our most gifted orators stood up and spoke to the
crowd, but there was one man who eclipsed everyone else. As that
man stood there, everybody was spellbound, electrified; and I—a
boy of eight years of age—was carried away with the marvelous
eloquence of this man. Years passed. One day, I went out on our
front lawn. I saw something lying on our lawn, all covered with
vomit, sleeping heavily, snoring like an overfed hog. When I went
up to it, I found that it was a man; and, alas, it was the very man
who had carried us all away on that steamer years before. He had
gone down. He died in a madhouse through drink and tobacco.

At our world's fair, a women's board was appointed to receive the dignitaries of the Old World, to receive the members of the nobility, and the members of the royalty of Spain and other countries. A woman stood right near Mrs. Potter Palmer, who was the ruling one of the women's commission, dazzling people by her beauty and wit. Just before I left Chicago to go round the world, some friends of mine were down in the slums of Chicago, hunting for poor, forlorn ones whom they might help, and they found a poor creature with nails grown like bird's claws; long, tangled hair, twisted and full of filth; and a face that had not been washed for weeks. She was clad in a single filthy garment—a wreck! And when they began to talk with her, they found she was that woman who had stood so near Mrs. Potter Palmer during all the honors of the world's fair. She had gone down through cocaine.

6. One thing more. Hell is a world without hope. There are men who tell you that the Greek word *aionios*, translated "everlasting," never means "everlasting"; but when they tell you so, either they have not looked into the matter, which is more likely, or else they tell you a deliberate falsehood. It is true that it does not necessarily mean "everlasting." Whether it does or does not has to be determined by the context. In Matthew 25:46, we read, *"These shall go away into everlasting punishment: but the righteous into life eternal"*; and if it means "everlasting" in one part of the verse, by every known law of exegesis, it must mean the same in the other part of the verse. Nobody questions that it does mean "everlasting" in the one case.

Furthermore, there is another expression, *"Eis tous aionas ton aionon"* ("Unto the ages of the ages"), used twelve times in one book: eight times, of the existence of God and the duration of His reign; once, of the duration of the blessedness of the righteous; and in every remaining instance, of the punishment of the beast, the false prophet, and the impenitent—the strongest known expression for absolute endlessness. Men, I have hunted my Bible through for one ray of hope for men who die impenitent, a ray of hope that can be called such when the passage is properly interpreted by the right laws of exegesis; and I have failed, after years of search, to find one. I am familiar with the passages men quote, but they will not bear the burden placed upon them when carefully interpreted in their context with an honest attempt to discover what they really mean, and not to make them fit a theory. The New Testament does not hold out one ray of hope for men and women who die without Christ. Anyone who does, dares to do what God has not done. *"For ever and ever"* is the never-ceasing wail of that restless sea of fire. Such is hell—a place of bodily anguish, a place of agony of conscience, a place of insatiable torment and desire, a place of evil companionship, a place of shame, and a place without hope.

How to Escape Hell

There is but one way to escape hell, that is, by accepting Jesus Christ as your personal Savior, surrendering to Him as your Lord and Master, openly confessing Him before the world, and demonstrating your faith through a life of obedience. The Bible is perfectly plain about that.

> *There is none other name under heaven given among men, whereby we must be saved.* (Acts 4:12)

> *He that believeth on the Son hath everlasting life: and he that believeth not the Son shall not see life; but the wrath of God abideth on him.* (John 3:36)

> *Whosoever therefore shall confess me before men, him will I confess also before my Father which is in heaven. But whosoever shall deny me before men, him will I also deny before my Father which is in heaven.* (Matthew 10:32–33)

The Lord Jesus shall be revealed from heaven with his mighty angels, in flaming fire taking vengeance on them that know not God, and that obey not the gospel of our Lord Jesus Christ: who shall be punished with everlasting destruction from the presence of the Lord, and from the glory of his power.

(2 Thessalonians 1:7–9)

The question is this: Will you accept Christ today? Men and women, hell is too awful to risk it a year; it is too awful to risk it a month; it is too awful to risk it a week; it is too awful to risk it a day. Our eternal destiny may be settled inside of twenty-four hours. It is too awful to risk it an hour. It is too awful to risk it till you have finished this chapter! Take Christ now. I know what some of you are saying, or what the devil is whispering to you. He is saying, "Don't be a coward. Don't be frightened into repentance." Men, is it cowardice to be moved by rational fear? Is it heroism to rush into unnecessary danger? Suppose I went outside and saw a building on fire and a man sitting at an upper window, reading a book carelessly. I see his peril, and I lift my hand to my mouth and say, "Flee for your life, the house is on fire." Then suppose that man should lean out the window and shout back, "I am no coward. You can't frighten me." Would he be playing the hero, or would he be playing the fool?

One night, I went to see my parents at the old home. They are both in heaven now. As I stepped off the train, I stepped onto another track. Unknown to me, an express train was coming down that other track. A cabman of the town saw my peril, put his hand to his mouth, and cried, "Mr. Torrey, there is a train coming—get off the track!" I did not shout back, "I am no coward; you can't scare me." I was not such a fool. I got off the track, or I would not be here today to tell the story.

Men and women, you are on the track; up the track, I hear the not-far-distant thunder and rumble of the wrath of God as it comes hurrying on, and I cry tonight, "Get off the track!" Take Christ tonight! Take Him now! If you are reasonable, you will. If you don't, you will not be playing the hero but playing the fool.

GOD'S BLOCKADE OF THE ROAD TO HELL

"The Lord is...not willing that any should perish, but that all should come to repentance."
—2 Peter 3:9

If any man or woman reading this is lost, it won't be God's fault. God does not wish you to be lost. God longs to have you saved. If God had His way, every man and woman reading this book would not only be saved sometime but saved right now. God is doing everything in His power to bring you men and women to repentance. Of course, He cannot save you if you will not repent. You can have salvation if you want to be saved from sin, but sin and salvation can never go together. There are people who talk about a scheme of salvation whereby man can continue in sin and yet be saved. It is impossible. Sin is damnation, and if a man will go on everlastingly in sin, he will be everlastingly lost.

But God is doing everything in His power to turn you out of the path of sin and destruction into the path of righteousness and everlasting life. God has filled the path of sin—the path that leads to hell—with obstacles. He has made it hard and bitter. A great many people today are saying, "The Christian life is so hard." It is not. "[Christ's] *yoke is easy, and* [His] *burden is light*" (Matthew 11:30). God tells us in His Word, "*The way of transgressors is hard*" (Proverbs 13:15). God has filled it full of obstacles, and you cannot go on in it without surmounting one obstacle after another. I am to talk to you about some of the obstacles that God has put in the path of sin and ruin.

The Bible

The first obstacle is the Bible. You cannot get very far in the path of sin without finding the Bible in your way. The Bible is one of the greatest hindrances to sin in the world. With its warnings; invitations; descriptions of the character and consequences of sin; representations of righteousness, beauty, and reward; and pictures of God and God's love, the Bible always stands as a great hindrance to sin. It makes men uneasy in sin. That is the reason many men hate the Bible; they are determined to sin, so they hate the Book.

Men will give you a great many reasons why they object to the Bible; but in ninety-nine cases out of a hundred, if you should trace men's objections to the Bible home, you would find the reason they hate the Bible is because it makes them uneasy in their sin. Men sometimes say to me, "I object to the Bible because of its filthy stories," but when I look into their lives, I find that they are filthy and that their real objection is not to filthy stories, of which there are none. There are stories of sin, stories that paint sin in its true colors, stories that make sin hideous—and their objection is not because of filthy stories but because the Bible makes them uneasy in their filthy lives.

This is why you hate the Bible: It makes it hard for you to go on in sin. How often a man has been turned back from the path of sin by a single verse in the Bible. Hundreds of men have been turned out of the path of sin by reading Romans 6:23: *"The wages of sin is death; but the gift of God is eternal life through Jesus Christ our Lord."* Thousands of men have been turned out of the path of sin by reading Amos 4:12: *"Prepare to meet thy God."* Tens of thousands of men have been turned out of the path of sin by reading John 3:16: *"For God so loved the world, that he gave his only begotten Son, that whosoever believeth in him should not perish, but have everlasting life,"* and by reading John 6:37: *"Him that cometh to me I will in no wise cast out."*

Several years ago, a man who had not been in a house of worship for fifteen or sixteen years came into our church in Chicago. He was a rampant infidel. I don't know why he came in that night. I suppose it was because he saw the crowd coming and was curious to know what was going on. He sat down, and I began to preach. In my sermon, I quoted John 6:37: *"Him that cometh to me I will in no wise cast out."* It went like an arrow into that man's heart. When the meeting was over, he got up and went out, and he tried to forget that verse but could not. He went to bed but could not sleep. *"Him that cometh to me I will in no wise cast out"* kept ringing in his mind.

It haunted him at work the next day, and then the next day and the next after that; for days and weeks, that verse haunted him, but he was bound not to come to Christ. He came back to the street where our church stands, walked up and down the sidewalk, stamped his foot, and cursed the text, but he could not get rid of it. Six weeks passed, and he came into our prayer meeting and said, "Men and women, I was here six weeks ago and heard your minister preach. I heard the text, John 6:37, and I have tried to forget it, but it has haunted me night and day. I have walked up and down the sidewalk in front of your church. I have stamped on the sidewalk and cursed the text, but I can't get rid of it. Pray for me." And we did, and he was saved. One text from God's Word turned him out of the path of sin and ruin.

A Mother's Holy Influence and Prayers

The second obstacle that God has put in the path of sin is a mother—her holy influence and teaching, as well as her prayers.

There are hundreds of men and women who are not yet Christians who have tried to be infidels, tried to plunge down into sin, but their mothers' holy influence and Christian teaching won't let them go the way they wish to. Sometimes, it is years afterward that a mother's teaching does its work.

In America, we had a young fellow who went west to Colorado in the mining times. He worked in the mines during the day and gambled at night, as so many miners do, but he spent more money gambling than he made in the mines. One night, he was at the gaming table and lost his last cent. Then he used some of his employer's money and lost that. He felt that he was ruined. He arose from the gaming table, went up into the mountains, drew his revolver, and held it to his temple; but as he was about to pull the trigger, a word that his mother had spoken to him years before came to his mind: "My son, if you are ever in trouble, think of God." And there, standing in the moonlight with a cocked revolver pressed against his temple and his finger upon the trigger, he remembered what his mother had said, dropped to his knees, cried out to God, and was saved. He was turned out of the path of perdition by his mother's teaching.

Another obstacle that God has put in the path of sin and ruin is a mother's prayers. Oh, men, in the desperate hardness of our hearts, we often trample our mother's teaching underfoot, but we find it very hard to get over her prayers. How often is a man saved at the last moment by his mother's prayers. In my church in Chicago, there was a man who stood outside the tabernacle with a pitcher of beer, and as the people came out of meetings, he would offer them drink. He was hard and desperate and wicked, but he had a praying mother in Scotland. Once, when he went home from the meeting where he had caused trouble, he was awakened in the middle of the night and saved without getting out of bed, all in answer to the prayers of a godly mother in Scotland. He went back to Scotland to see his mother. He had a brother who was a sailor in the China Seas, and the mother and the saved son knelt down and prayed for the wandering boy; and that very night while they prayed, the Spirit of God came down upon that sailor, and he was saved. Afterward, he became Dr. Morrison, a missionary to India—saved by a mother's prayers.

I stand here today a saved man because, when I was rushing headlong in the path of sin and ruin, my mother's prayers arose; and I could not get over them. I used to think that nobody had anything to do with my salvation, no living being, for I was awakened in the middle of the night. I had gone to bed with no more thought of becoming a Christian than I had of jumping over the moon. In the middle of the night, I jumped out of bed and started to end my miserable life. But something came upon me, and I dropped on my knees; and in five minutes from the time I got out of bed to take my life, I had surrendered to God. I thought no man or woman had anything to do with it, but I found out a woman had—my mother—four hundred and twenty-seven miles away, praying; and while I had gotten over sermons and arguments and churches and everything else, I could not get over my mother's prayers. Do you know why some of you are not in hell already? Your mother's prayers have kept you out of hell.

Sermons

Another obstacle is the sermons we hear. How many thousands and tens of thousands of men have turned from sin to God by sermons that they heard or read? Sometimes, the sermon does its work years afterward.

I remember once, in my first pastorate, I prepared a sermon on the parable of the ten virgins. There was one woman in my congregation who was very much on my heart, and I prayed that she might be saved by that sermon. I fully expected to see her saved, but when I gave out the invitation, she never made a sign. I went home and did not know what to make of it. I said, "I prayed for her salvation by that sermon and fully expected her to be saved, and she is not saved. I don't know what to make of it." Years afterward, when I had gone to another pastorate, I heard that this woman was saved. I revisited the place and called upon her, saying, "I am very glad to hear you have been converted." She said, "Would you like to know how I was converted?" I said I would. "Do you remember preaching a sermon years ago on the ten virgins? When you preached that sermon, I could not get it out of my mind. I felt I must take Christ that night, but I would not, and that sermon followed me, and I was converted years after by that sermon"—the sermon I was sure she was going to be saved by. But I did not see it for years.

The Influence and Teaching of a Sunday School Teacher

Another obstacle is a Sunday school teacher's influence and teaching. How many people do we know who were brought to Christ by the teaching of a faithful Christian man or woman in Sunday school? I want to say to all you teachers that a faithful Sunday school teacher is one of God's best instruments on earth for the salvation of the perishing.

Mr. Moody's first Sunday school in Chicago was full of very unruly girls—nobody could manage them—but finally, he found a young man who could manage them. One day, this man came into

Mr. Moody's shop (it was before Mr. Moody went out of business) and said, "Mr. Moody." Then he burst into tears. Mr. Moody said, "What is the matter?" "The doctor says I have consumption and that I must go to California at once, or I'll die," and he sobbed as if his heart would break. Mr. Moody tried to comfort him, saying, "Suppose that is so. You have no occasion to feel so bad. You are a Christian." "It is not that, Mr. Moody; I am perfectly willing to die, I am not afraid to die; but here, I have had this Sunday school class all these years, and not one of the students have been saved, and I am going off to leave them." And he sobbed like a child. Mr. Moody said, "Wait. I will get a carriage, and we will drive around and visit them, and, one by one, you can lead them to Christ."

He took the pale teacher in the carriage, and they drove around to the homes of the girls, and he talked to them about Christ until he was so tired that he had to be taken home. The next day, they went out again, and they went out every day until every one of these young women but one was saved. Then they met for a prayer meeting before he went away. One after another led in prayer, and, at last, the one unsaved girl in the whole company led in prayer, too, and accepted Christ. He left by the early train the next morning, and Mr. Moody went down to the train to see him off. As they were waiting, the girls dropped in one by one, without prearranging their visitation, until every one of the young women was on the platform. He spoke a few words of farewell to them, and as the train pulled out of the station, he stood upon the back platform of the car with his finger pointing heavenward, telling his Sunday school class to meet him in heaven.

A Kind Word or an Act of God

A kind word or an act God often throws as an obstacle in the path of sin. My friend was standing in a window looking out on Bleecker Street, New York, when a drunkard came down the street. He had been a man in high circumstances, the mayor of a Southern city, but he had gone down through drink and was now a penniless drunkard. He had made up his mind to commit suicide. He started for the river, but as he was going down Bleecker Street, he thought, *I will go into a public house and have one more drink. I have spent a lot of money in that bar, and I can certainly stand the man off for one drink.* He went in and asked for a drink, telling the man he had no money to pay for it; and the man came around from behind the bar and kicked him into the gutter.

Looking out the window, my friend saw the poor wretch picking himself up out of the gutter. She crossed over, wiped the mud off with her handkerchief, and said, "Come over in there. It is bright and warm, and you will be welcome," and the poor wretch went over and sat down behind the stove. The meeting began, and one person after another gave his testimony; and when the meeting was over, my friend came and spoke to him about his soul. His heart was touched, and he was saved.

This saved man secured a job and then a better one, and finally he was made manager of one of the largest publishing houses in the city of New York. One day, he came to my friend and said, "I have some friends down at a hotel; I want you to meet them." She went to the hotel, and he introduced her to a fine-looking middle-aged woman and a fine-looking young lady, saying, "This is my wife and daughter"—beautiful, refined, cultured ladies whom he had left and gone down to the very verge of hell; but a kind act and a word of invitation to Christ had turned him from the path to perdition to the path that leads to glory, all when he was within one step of hell. Oh, let us go as the missionaries of God's grace and block the path of sinful men and women with kindly deeds, thus turning them to righteousness and to God.

The Work of the Holy Spirit

Another obstacle that God puts in the path of sin and ruin is the work of the Holy Spirit. How strange it is. You and I have experienced it. When we were right in the midst of carousing, a strange feeling came into our heart—an unrest; a dissatisfaction with the life we were living; a longing for something better; memories of home, church, mother, Bible, and God.

One night, a man was playing cards at the table. He was a man wholly given up to the world, belonging to one of your noble families—not a nobleman himself, but connected with members of the nobility. A wild, reckless English spendthrift, there he sat, playing cards. Suddenly, the voice of God's Spirit spoke in his heart, and he thought he was about to die. He sprang up from the table, threw down his cards, and rushed to his room. There was someone in the room. He thought at first, *It won't do to pray while the maid is in the room.* But he was so much in earnest that he did not mind her presence. He dropped down by his bed and called upon God, for Christ's sake, to forgive his sins.

That man was Brownlow North, who did such a great work for God in Ireland and Scotland in 1759 and 1760. Oh, friends, listen. Last night, as you were in some den of infamy, there came into your heart a wretchedness, a sense of self-disgust, a longing for something better, a calling to a purer life—what was it? God's Spirit. Perhaps right now, there is a stirring in your heart, and you are saying to yourself, "I wonder if I had better not become a Christian today." Almost a determination to stand up as soon as the invitation is given out. What is it? God sending His Spirit to blockade the road to hell. Listen, men—listen to God's Spirit today. Yield and accept Christ.

The Cross of Christ

Another obstacle that God has put in the road as a blockade in the path to hell is the cross of Christ. No man can get very far down the path of sin and ruin until he sees looming before him the cross. On that cross, there hangs a Man—the Son of Man, the Son of God. There you see Him hanging, with nails in His hands and feet, and He says, "It was for you. I bore this for you. I died for you." Oh, men, in the pathway of every man and woman stands the cross with Christ upon it, and if you go out to continue in sin, you will have to go over the cross and over the crucified form of the Son of God.

I heard of a godly old man who had a worthless son. That son was more anxious to make money than he was for honor or anything else, and he determined to go into that infamous business in which there is lots of money but in which no self-respecting man will undertake—the liquor business. Well, this man so far lost his self-respect that he was going to open a bar, and his father was ashamed. He pled with him. He said, "My boy, you bear an honored name which has never before been disgraced. Don't disgrace it by putting it up over a bar." But the son was so bent on making money that he would not listen to his father's voice.

The day came to open the bar. The father was about the first on hand. He stood outside the door of that bar, and he told every man who approached the door of the miseries that come from strong drink, warned him of the consequences of entering such a place as that; and, one after another, they turned away. The son looked out the window to see why he was getting no customers. He saw his father outside, turning his customers away. So, he went out and said, "Father, go home. You are ruining my business." His father replied, "I cannot help it, my boy. I won't have my name dishonored by this business; and if you are bent on going on with it, I will stand here and warn every man who comes to enter your door." Finally, the son lost his temper. He struck his old father. I tell you, friends, this liquor business will take the humanity out of people—he struck his old father in the face. The father turned to him without the least bit of anger. He said, "My son, you can strike me if you will; you can kill me if you will, but no man shall enter your bar unless he goes over my dead body."

Men, listen! No man or woman will ever enter hell unless by going over the dead body of Jesus Christ. No man or woman can go out refusing Christ, persisting in sin, without trampling underfoot the form of Him who was crucified on the cross of Calvary for you.

Oh, men, God has piled the obstacles so high in His patient love! Don't try to surmount them. Turn back. Turn out of the path of sin; turn into the path of faith in Jesus Christ. Turn now!

5

HEAVEN: WHAT SORT OF PLACE IT IS AND HOW TO GET THERE

*"He looked for a city which hath foundations, whose builder
and maker is God."*
—Hebrews 11:10

"Here have we no continuing city, but we seek one to come."
—Hebrews 13:14

"I go to prepare a place for you."
—John 14:2

*"And God shall wipe away all tears from their eyes; and there
shall be no more death, neither sorrow, nor crying, neither shall
there be any more pain: for the former things are passed away."*
—Revelation 21:4

My subject in this chapter is what sort of place heaven is and how to get there. This was the city Abraham sought, the *"city which hath foundations"* (Hebrews 11:10), the *"continuing city"* (Hebrews 13:14), which we are seeking over the fleeting and perishable cities and homes of earth.

What sort of place is heaven? In answer to this question, I am not going to tell what sort of a place I imagine heaven to be. I care very little for my speculations or any other man's speculations and fancies on this point. I am going to tell you something that is sure about it. I am going to tell you what God plainly teaches about it in His Word. There are many who think we know nothing about heaven, that it is all guesswork. That is not so. God has revealed to us very much about it, and what He has revealed about it is very cheering and eminently calculated to awaken in every wise and true heart a desire to go there. I think that if we reflected more on heaven, it would help us to bear our burdens here more bravely; it would incite us to holier living; it would do much to deliver us from the power of the greed and the lust that is blighting so many lives; it would make us cheerier and more sunshiny. Those are very shallow philosophers who tell us that our present business is to live this present life and let the future take care of itself. You might as well tell the schoolboy that his present business is to live today and take no outlook into the future life of manhood, that he might wisely prepare for it on the one hand and feel its stimulus on the other. True thoughts of the life that is to come clothe the life that now is with new beauty and strength. Let us then think awhile about heaven. What do we know about it?

What Sort of a Place Is Heaven?

First of all, heaven is a place. Jesus said, *"I go to prepare a **place** for you"* (John 14:2). Some will tell you that heaven is merely a state or a condition. Doubtless, it is more important to be in a heavenly state or condition than in a heavenly place. It would unquestionably be preferable to be in hell in a heavenly state of thought and heart than to be in heaven in a hellish state of thought and heart. But heaven is a place. We are not to be merely in a heavenly state of mind but in a heavenly city, as well, *"a city which hath foundations"* (Hebrews 11:10), a *"continuing city"* (Hebrews 13:14). Christ has already entered into heaven now to appear in the presence of God for us. (See Hebrews 9:24.) He has gone to prepare a place for us, and He is coming back for us to take us to it. We are not to be disembodied spirits in the world to come but redeemed spirits in redeemed bodies, in a redeemed society, and in a redeemed universe.

Internal and External Beauty

Heaven is a place of incomparable beauty, both external and internal. This truth appears from such descriptions as we have in Revelation 21–22. The God of the Bible is a God of beauty. He made this world beautiful, but its beauty has been marred by sin—the weeds, thorns, and briers spring up; the insects devour the roses; the lilies fade; and decay and death bring loathsome sights and foul smells. *"The whole creation"* (Romans 8:22), fallen in sympathy with fallen man, groans and travails together in pain until now. But enough is left of the primal beauty to show us how intensely God loves beauty, and He has told us in His Word that creation itself shall be delivered from the bondage of corruption and be given the glorious liberty of the children of God. (See Romans 8:21.)

There will be in heaven the perfection of beauty—perfection of form, color, sound, and odor. The beauty that is to be is necessarily indescribable. All earthly comparisons necessarily fail. Every sense and faculty of perception in our present state is blunted by sin and the disease that results from sin. But, in our redeemed bodies, every sense and faculty will receive enlargement and exist in perfection. What new senses there may be, we cannot, of course, imagine. Every faculty will have unlimited opportunity for exercise. The highest and most faultless material beauty, the counterpart and double of the moral beauty of that world, will surround us on every side, filling eyes and ears and nostrils. Some of us have seen beautiful visions on earth. We have seen the mountains rearing their snow-crowned heads through the clouds; we have seen the vista of rolling hills and verdant valleys and winding rivers and forests with their changing colors; we have seen the lake and ocean dancing and tossing and rolling in the moonlight; we have seen the heavens in the clear, wintry night, bejeweled with their countless stars; we have caught the fragrances that float through the summer night in park and garden and tropical island; we have listened to the indescribable harmonies of piano and violin and organ as they responded to the touch of the master's hand; and we have heard the more matchless music of the human voice; but all these are nothing to the beauty of sight and sound and fragrance that will greet us in that fair *"city which hath foundations."* This shall be the lot of the poorest of God's children. That poor widow who tonight toils by the dim candlelight to gain the pitifully small wage with which pitiless sweaters reward her painful toil will soon be at rest and will enter upon these scenes of indescribable beauty, to go no more out forever.

High, Holy, and Ennobling Companionships

However, the beauty of heaven, as good and attractive as it is, will be its least important characteristic. Heaven will be a place of high, holy, and ennobling companionships. The best and wisest and noblest men of all ages will be there. Abraham and Isaac and Jacob will be there. Jesus said, *"And I say unto you, That many shall* come from the east and west, and shall sit down with Abraham, and Isaac, and Jacob, in the kingdom of heaven" (Matthew 8:11). Moses, Elijah, Daniel, Paul, and John; Rutherford, Brainerd, and Payson; all the purest, noblest, most unselfish men and women the world has known; all those who have trusted in the atoning blood of Christ ("For we know that if our earthly house of this tabernacle were dissolved, we have a building of God, an house not made with hands, eternal in the heavens" [2 Corinthians 5:1]); all the dear ones who believed in and loved the Lord Jesus—all will be there.

There are many who desire to get into the best society of earth. That is all right if it really is the best society and not merely the society of wealth and fashion and foolishness that is sometimes so strangely and irrationally called "the best society." But the very best society of this world will be nothing to the society of heaven. The joys we find in the companionship of noble, unselfish, thoughtful people here, in the dearest companionships we know, give but the faintest conception of the joys of heaven's companionships.

The angels are there. (See Luke 1:19; 15:7, 10.) We shall enjoy the companionship of these lofty intelligences, every one—Gabriel, Michael, and the whole angelic host.

God Himself is there, too. In a sense, He is everywhere; but heaven is the place of His peculiar presence and manifestation of Himself. "Then hear thou from heaven thy dwelling place" (2 Chronicles 6:30). "Thy kingdom come. Thy will be done in earth, as it is in heaven" (Matthew 6:10). We shall hold communion with Him.

Jesus Christ is there. "And said, Behold, I see the heavens opened, and the Son of man standing on the right hand of God" (Acts 7:56). "Seeing then that we have a great high priest, that is passed into the heavens, Jesus the Son of God, let us hold fast our profession" (Hebrews 4:14). "Now of the things which we have spoken this is the sum: We

*have such an high priest, who is set on the right hand of the throne of
the Majesty in the heavens"* (Hebrews 8:1).

To Paul, this was one of the most attractive thoughts about
heaven. *"But I am in a strait betwixt the two, having the desire to
depart and be with Christ; for it is very far better"* (Philippians 1:23
RV). The holy Rutherford also cried, "I would rather be in hell with
Thee than in heaven without Thee; for, if I were in hell with Thee,
that would be heaven to me; and if I were in heaven without Thee,
that would be hell to me."

On the other hand, there will be no unpleasant or degrading
companionships there. The devil will not be there. The lewd, the
vulgar, and the obscene will not be there. The avaricious and the
scheming and the selfish will not be there. The liar and the slan-
derer and the backbiter and the meddler and the gossip will not be
there. The mean and the contemptible and the hypocrite will not
be there. The profane and the blasphemer and the infidel and the
scoffer will not be there. No money or influence or cunning will
get them in. *"And there shall in no wise enter into it any thing that
defileth, neither whatsoever worketh abomination, or maketh a lie: but
they which are written in the Lamb's book of life"* (Revelation 21:27).
It will be a good place to be. Birmingham would not be such a bad
place to live in if we could get rid of some of its inhabitants. All
such will be gotten rid of there. There are limitations to the joys of
the dearest earthly companionships. Here,

> Thought is deeper than all speech;
> Feeling deeper than all thought;
> Souls to souls can never teach
> What unto themselves was taught.[2]

It will not be so there. We can perfectly open our hearts to one
another there, as we so often and so vainly long to do here. *"For*

2. Christopher Pearse Cranch, "Gnosis."

now we see through a glass, darkly; but then face to face: now I know in part; but then shall I know even as also I am known" (1 Corinthians 13:12).

Heaven will be a place of glad reunions. *"Then we which are alive and remain shall be caught up together with them* [those who have left us] *in the clouds, to meet the Lord in the air: and so shall we ever be with the Lord"* (1 Thessalonians 4:17). The bereaved wife shall meet again the husband she has missed so long. The son shall meet again the mother whose departure left his life so desolate. There we shall meet again children who were removed from us in all the beauty of their early life, and whom we have never forgotten through all the months and years that have passed since. Ah! What glad days they will be when we meet again, never more to part.

Free from Curses That Mar Life

Heaven will be a place that is free from everything that curses or mars our life here. The world we live in would be a happy place indeed if it were not for a few things. If there were no sin, no sickness, no pain, no poverty, no servile labor, no want, and no death, this world would be good. But these things mar and well-nigh ruin this present world. There will be none of these things in heaven. There will be no sin; everyone will perfectly obey the will of God. There will be no poverty; everyone will have all the inexhaustible wealth of God at his disposal. *"And if* [we are] *children, then heirs; heirs of God, and joint-heirs with Christ; if so be that we suffer with him, that we may be also glorified together"* (Romans 8:17).

There will be no servile, grinding toil. I tell you, when I see weary women who toil from early morn until late at night over the tub or ironing board or sewing machine, when I see the men who rise at break of day and go forth to the forge or bench or ditch, I rejoice that there is a place where the weary are at rest. There will be none of these things in heaven. "*There remaineth therefore a rest to the people of God*" (Hebrews 4:9).

There will be neither sickness nor pain. "*And God shall wipe away all tears from their eyes; and there shall be no more death, neither sorrow, nor crying, neither shall there be any more pain: for the former things are passed away*" (Revelation 21:4). No more aching limbs, no more throbbing temples, no more darting pains, no more grinding tortures, no more swelling tongues, no more weakness, no more sighs, no more groans, no more nights of tossing in sweltering rooms, no more tears. There will be no death in heaven. No breaking hearts as we look at the ashen faces and glazed eyes of loved ones for the last time. No watching the undertaker as he screws down the coffin lid on the one we loved. There will be no black dresses and veils, no funerals passing through the streets, no standing by a yawning grave and watching a coffin lowered into it, no listening to the cold clods as they fall remorselessly on the box that contains the form of the one we love so much and whose departure leaves life so cheerless. Thank God there is no death in heaven.

Universal and Perfect Knowledge

Heaven will be a place of universal and perfect knowledge. Here, the wisest of us sees God through a glass darkly, but there we will see Him face-to-face; here we know Him in part, but there we will know Him even as we are known. (See 1 Corinthians 13:12.) The wisest scientist or philosopher on earth knows but very little. The little he knows is exceedingly precious, but it is very little. When Sir Isaac Newton was an old man, he said to one who praised his wisdom, "I am as a child on the seashore picking up a pebble here and a shell there, but the great ocean of truth still lies before me." In heaven, the most uneducated of us will have fathomed that great ocean of truth. Perfect knowledge of all things.

The great perplexing problems of God and man, of time and eternity, solved. God's wondrous purposes and their accomplishment lying open before us. No doubts, no questionings, no uncertainties, no errors. Faith swallowed up in sight.

Universal and Perfect Love

Heaven will be a place of universal and perfect love. *"Beloved, now are we the sons of God, and it doth not yet appear what we shall be: but we know that, when he shall appear, we shall be like him; for we shall see him as he is"* (1 John 3:2). We shall be like Him who is love. *"He that loveth not knoweth not God; for God is love"* (1 John 4:8). What a place to live, where everyone is a lover and where all love is perfect. How happy is the home where love is triumphant. It may be a lowly home, a very plain place, but it is a happy place. *"Better is a dinner of herbs where love is, than a stalled ox and hatred therewith"* (Proverbs 15:17). All is love there. And the love there will not be like that of earth—hesitating, suspicious, changeful, selfish, so cold and then so warm—but pure, unbounded, unfaltering, unchanging, constant, and Christlike. What a world that will be! The universal brotherhood of which we read and talk so much and of which we see so little will find its perfect realization there.

A Place of Praise

Heaven will be a place of praise.

After this I beheld, and, lo, a great multitude, which no man could number, of all nations, and kindreds, and people, and tongues, stood before the throne, and before the Lamb, clothed with white robes, and palms in their hands; and cried with a loud voice, saying, Salvation to our God which sitteth upon the throne, and unto the Lamb. And all the angels stood round about the throne, and about the elders and the four beasts,

*and fell before the throne on their faces, and worshipped God,
saying, Amen: Blessing, and glory, and wisdom, and thanks-
giving, and honor, and power, and might, be unto our God for
ever and ever. Amen.* (Revelation 7:9–12)

Men will have open eyes to see God as He is. To see Jesus
Christ as He is. Souls will throb and burst forth with praise.
Suppose we should get one glimpse of God as He is, one view of
Jesus Christ as He is! There would be a burst of song rising such
as never rang before. There will be melody all day long in heaven.
Some people ask me in a critical way, "Why do you have so much
music in your meetings?" Because we wish them to be like heaven
as much as possible. Heaven will be a very musical place. There
will be far more singing than preaching there.

A City with Foundations

Heaven will be *"a city which hath foundations"* (Hebrews 11:10),
a *"continuing city"* (Hebrews 13:14). Earth's greatest cities and
earth's fairest homes do not abide; they crumble into dust. The so-
called eternal city of the past is trodden underneath the unheed-
ing feet of the beggars of modern Rome. The world itself does not
abide. *"The world passeth away"* (1 John 2:17). Heaven does abide.
We enter it to go out no more, forever. The eons of eternity roll on,
but heaven abides in its beauty, in its glory, in its joyousness, and in
its love; and we abide with it.

How to Gain Entrance into Heaven

Is no heart stirred with a longing for that *"better country"*
(Hebrews 11:16)? Who would not rather have an entrance there
than to have the poor, fleeting possessions of any of earth's mil-
lionaires? If I had my choice between having all that money could

buy, including the most splendid mansion on earth, and living in the most wretched tenement in want and hunger and suffering all my days in order to gain heaven, it would not take long for me to choose. Ah, when we reach that fair home, the privations of earth through which we may have passed will seem small and trifling indeed. *"I reckon that the sufferings of this present time are not worthy to be compared with the glory which shall be revealed in us"* (Romans 8:18). But we may all gain an entrance there.

There is but one way, yet that is very simple and open to all. *"Jesus saith unto [Thomas], I am the way, the truth, and the life: no man cometh unto the Father, but by me."* He also said, *"I am the door: by me if any man enter in, he shall be saved, and shall go in and out, and find pasture"* (John 10:9). Christ is the door to heaven; He is the way to God. Accept Christ—accept Him fully as your Savior, your Master, and your Lord. Do it right now. If you stood outside the door of some fair mansion tonight, where all inside was beauty, sociability, joyousness, and love, and, with cordial invitation, the owner said, "Come in," would you wait for a second invitation and risk it not being given? But even now, Jesus swings heaven's door open wide and says, "Come in." Accept Him at once and gain a right to enter and live forever in heaven.

Over in our country, there was a godless father who had a sweet little child who was an earnest Christian. This young daughter fell ill and died. The father was very angry at God. After the funeral, he raged about his room, cursing God for taking his beloved child from him. At last, utterly worn out, he threw himself upon the bed and fell asleep. In his slumber, he dreamed that he stood beside a dark river, across which he saw a beautiful land on the farther side. As he gazed across the river, he saw children's forms coming toward him. One fair child came forth, whom he soon recognized as his own little daughter. She was beckoning to him and calling, "Come over here, Father; come over here." He awoke and, bursting into tears, gave up his rebellion against God, accepted Christ, and prepared to meet his child in the fair land beyond the river.

Many of us hear voices of our loved ones who have gone before, calling, "Come over here, Father"; "Come over here, Mother"; "Come over here, Son"; "Come over here, Daughter"; "Come over here, Husband"; "Come over here, Wife." Let us accept Christ at once, and thus gain the right to enter heaven and live there forever.

THE NEW BIRTH

"Ye must be born again."
—John 3:7

No one can be saved unless he is born again by the power of God's Holy Spirit. *"Ye must be born again,"* Jesus said. The necessity is absolute; He did not say, *"Ye may be born again"* but *"Ye must be born again."*

Nothing else will take the place of the new birth. Neither baptism nor confirmation will take the place of the new birth. In the eighth chapter of the Acts of the Apostles, Simon was baptized; and whatever the right form of water baptism may be, he was baptized the right way, for he was baptized by a man sent by the apostles, and taken into the early church. But when Peter and John came down and saw Simon's heart, Peter said unto him, *"Thou hast neither part nor lot in this matter: for thy heart is not right in the sight* of God...*thou art still in the gall of bitterness, and in the bond of iniq-uity*" (Acts 8:21, 23). A baptized lost sinner! I go to people in these meetings and ask them to come to Christ, but they say, "I have been baptized; I have been confirmed." Have you been born again? *"Ye must be born again."*

No performance of religious duties will take the place of the new birth. A great many people are depending upon the fact that they say their prayers, read their Bibles, go to church, partake of the sacrament, and perform other duties; but all that will not take the place of the new birth. *"Ye must be born again."*

Orthodoxy of faith will not take the place of the new birth. A great many people are saying, "I believe the Apostles' Creed"; "I believe the Nicene Creed"; "I believe in the Larger and Shorter Catechism"; "I am orthodox and hold the right views about Christ, the Bible, and the atonement." You can be orthodox upon every doctrine and be lost forever. I suppose the devil is as orthodox as a person can get. The devil knows the truth about the Bible. He hates the Bible and loves to get others to believe something else, but he believes it himself. The devil knows the truth about Christ. He believes in the divinity of Christ. He tries to keep others from believing in it, but he believes in it himself—he knows Jesus Christ is divine. The devil believes the truth about hell. There is no one who knows better than the devil that there is an everlasting hell. The devil is perfectly orthodox, but he is lost. *"Ye must be born again."*

Culture, refinement, and outward correctness of life will not take the place of the new birth. The trouble with us is not merely in our outward life. The trouble is in the heart. The corruption is in the heart, in the very deepest depths of our inner life. To merely reform your outward life is not enough, because it does not go deep enough. Suppose I had a rotten apple. I could take that apple to an artist and have him put a coating of wax around it and then paint it until it was just as beautiful in appearance as any apple you ever saw, but it would still be just as rotten as ever. Take one bite into it, and you bite into the decay. The trouble with you is that out of Christ, you are rotten at the heart, and mere culture, refinement, respectability, reform, and morality are simply putting a coating of wax on the outside and painting it up. Change must reach the deepest depths of your being. What we need is the power of God going down to the deepest depths of our souls, banishing death and bringing in life, banishing corruption and bringing in the holiness of God. *"Follow…holiness, without which no man shall see the Lord"* (Hebrews 12:14). It is only by the regenerating power of the Spirit of God that men and women are made holy. *"Ye must be born again."*

The necessity of the new birth is universal. There is not a man or a woman on the face of the earth who shall ever see the kingdom of God, or enter the kingdom of God, except he or she be born again. There is no exception. There is not a woman in Birmingham—I care not how refined, how highly educated, how amiable, how beautiful in her daily life she is—who will ever see the kingdom of God unless she is born again.

If anybody could have entered the kingdom of God without the new birth, it was Nicodemus. Nicodemus was an upright man, honored by everyone; a man of wealth and culture, he moved in the best society. He belonged to the orthodox party, a man of deep religious earnestness, sincerely desiring to know the right way. He was a man who prayed and studied his Bible, and he went regularly to the synagogue, several times a week. One day, the Lord Jesus looked him right in the face and said, "Nicodemus, you must be born again." No exceptions. *"Except a man be born again, he cannot see the kingdom of God."*

So, I come to you with the question, "Have you been born again?" I do not ask if you are a church member. I do not ask you if you believe the truth. I do not ask if you say your prayers or read your Bible. I do not ask if you go to church. I do not ask if you have a liberal heart toward the poor. I do not ask if you give to foreign missions. Have you been born again?

"Well," somebody says, "what does it mean to be born again?" As good a definition of the new birth as I know is given in 2 Corinthians 5:17: "*If any man be in Christ, he is a new creature [creation]: old things are passed away; behold, all things are become new.*" The new birth is a new creation—a radical transformation by the power of the Spirit of God in the deepest depths of our being; a new will, new affections, new thoughts.

Transformation of the Will, Affection, and Taste

We are born with a perverted will. We are born with corrupted affections. We are born with a blinded mind. In regeneration by the power of the Holy Spirit, God transforms our will, affections, and tastes—our way of looking at things. Let me explain it a little better. Every man and woman has, by nature, a perverted will—a will that is set on pleasing self. By nature, we love to please ourselves. What pleases us may not be vicious at all—we may not be pleased to get drunk or swear or lie or do anything vicious or vulgar—but our minds are bent on pleasing ourselves. Yet when God, by His Spirit, imparts to us His nature and life, then our will and the whole purpose of our lives are changed. Instead of pleasing self, we set out to please God; the whole will is surrendered to God, and we live to please Him. We may do many of the things we did before, but now we do them because they please God. Before, we did them because they pleased ourselves.

Our affections are corrupt by nature. We love the things we ought not to love and hate the things we ought to love. For example, many women love to read novels more than they love to read the Bible. If a great many of these women were to tell the truth, they would say, "I would rather read a novel any day of the week than read the Bible." You love to go out dancing. I don't say God hates dancing, mind you; but He hates when we love it more than spending time with Him. God hates gambling—I am sure He does. You all would probably hate it, too, if you knew as much about it as I do. But you love to gamble; you would rather go out dancing than go to the gathering of God's children. If you had your choice between going somewhere to dance or going someplace where God's Spirit was present in power, you would probably choose dancing. You would go to a casino rather than to a quiet gathering of God's people where they knelt down and prayed for the outpouring of the Spirit.

When God, through the power of the Spirit, imparts to you a new nature, you will love the Bible more than any other book in the world. You will love the place where God manifests Himself better than any place of worldly entertainment. You will love the company of God's people better than you will love the pleasures of this world. And the beautiful thing is that, in a moment of time, by the power of God's Holy Spirit, the change comes.

New tastes and new affections take the place of old tastes and old affections. Not many people love the theater more than I once did, and the dance—I used to go to from four to six dances a week. Not many people love the casino more than I once did, for I played cards every day of my life except the Sabbath (I thank God that my mother's training kept me from doing it on the Sabbath day). You could not hire me to do these things today. I think there is not money enough in Birmingham to hire me to go to out dancing, unless I went there to get some poor soul out. There is not money enough in Birmingham to get me to play whist or casino or bridge or anything else. I hate it. I love the things I once hated, and I hate the things I once loved. Why, in those days, I would rather have read any novel than read the Bible. Today, I have more joy in reading my Bible than in any other book on earth. I love it. My greatest intellectual joy is just to pore over the wonderful pages of this book of God.

Then you will get new thoughts. A great many of you today are blind to the divine authority of this Book. You believe all the nonsense that people tell you, in the name of what they call "scholarship," about the mistakes in it. But when you are born again, you will get a mind so in tune with the mind of God that you will believe everything in it, in spite of everybody. Some of you cannot believe the doctrine of the atonement—that Jesus took our sins in His own body on the cross. The preaching of this doctrine is "foolishness to them that perish" (See 1 Corinthians 1:18); but when you are born again, the doctrine that the Son of God died on the cross of Calvary will be one of the sweetest doctrines in all the universe.

A new will set upon pleasing God instead of pleasing self, new affections to love the things that God loves and to hate the things that God hates, a new mind about the truth of God—have you been born again? If not, you are not saved. *"Verily, verily, I say unto thee, Except a man be born again, he cannot see the kingdom of God"* (John 3:3).

Practicing Righteousness

How can we tell whether we have been born again? *"Every one that doeth righteousness is born of him"* (1 John 2:29). If you have been born of God, you will do as God does. God does righteousness. If you are born of God, righteousness will be the practice of your life. What is righteousness? Doing that which is right in God's sight. A man who is born of God will study the Word of God to find out what God's will is, as revealed in His Word;

and when he finds out, he will do it. Are you doing that? Are you studying the Word of God daily to find out what God wants you to do? And then, when you find out what God wants you to do, are you doing it?

"Whosoever is born of God doth not commit sin" (1 John 3:9)— that is, does not make a practice of sinning. John tells us what he means by "sin" a few verses before this one. To commit sin is to do what you know to be contrary to God's will. When he knows God's will, the man of God will not disobey it. He may do something that he did not think at the time was not God's will, but he will find out it was not; and when he does, he will own up and confess it as sin. Or, he may be suddenly surprised, be overtaken by a sudden temptation, and fall; but, as soon as he sees it, he will confess it. He will not go on, day after day, doing that which he knows to be contrary to the will of God. Anybody who is making a practice, day after day, of something that he knows, when he does it, to be contrary to the will of God has reason to doubt whether he is born again.

A young man asked me on the street on Thursday, "If a man is born again and lies down in sin and dies in sin, will he be saved?" "Why," I said, "a man who is born again will not lie down in sin. He may fall into it, but he will not stay there."

Do you know the difference between a hog and a sheep? A hog will fall into the mud and stay there. A sheep may fall into the mud, but it gets up as quick as it can. A good many people who seem to be Christ's sheep are only washed sows. A sow that is washed will return to the mire, but a sheep will not stay in the mud. Some of you say, "I wish Dr. Torrey would not use such inelegant language." It is not my language, it is God's. If you are reformed only outwardly, if you are converted simply externally, then in a few weeks, you will go back to your sin and your worldliness. You are only a washed hog. I am quoting Scripture. It is God's language.

(See 2 Peter 2:22.) It is the person who is outwardly converted but not inwardly transformed who will give up after a little while; but if you have been born again, you are transformed from a sow into a sheep, and you will never again lie down in sin.

Loving Brothers and Sisters

In 1 John 3:14, we find the third proof of regeneration—love for brothers and sisters. *"We know that we have passed from death unto life, because we love the brethren."* Love of everybody who belongs to Christ, irrespective of social position, irrespective of race or color. *"We love the brethren,"* says every child of God. The nature of God is love, and if God has imparted His nature to you, then you have a heart full of love, and especially love for God's children.

I once went to a Communion service in the city of Brooklyn, and they were receiving new members. A lady sat near me, and when the people stood up to receive the new members, I saw that she did not stand up. When the meeting was over, I said to her—for I knew her very well—"Why didn't you stand up to receive the new members?" She replied, "I was not going to stand up for them. They are our mission people. I am not going to love and watch over and care for them." They were poor, and she was rich. She loved rich Christians. She was not a child of God.

You will love the poor old washerwoman who is born of God just as much as if she were the wife of a millionaire. You will love a woman who cannot read or write just as much as if she were the most highly educated woman in the kingdom. It is a practical love, a love that shows itself by digging in the pockets. People will sometimes get up in a prayer meeting and say, "I know I have passed from death to life because I love the brethren."

After the meeting, a lady goes around and says, "There is Mrs. Smith; she is in trouble. She needs a little help, and we are making up a little purse for her. Won't you give something?" And a woman replies, saying, "I cannot do it. Christmas is coming, and I have got to get presents for my sisters and children and cousins, and I cannot give to everybody." If woman is a child of God, she can give, for she does have it to give.

The Bible is such a practical Book, applicable to our everyday life. The proof of the new birth is love, and the proof of love is that you go and share the penny you have left in your pocket with your poor brothers and poor sisters.

Belief in Jesus Christ

Another test to see if we are born again is faith in Jesus Christ. *"Whosoever believeth that Jesus is the Christ is born of God"* (1 John 5:1). Now, you say, "I come in on that. I believe that Jesus is the Christ." Do you? "Of course, I do. I am perfectly orthodox." It is not orthodoxy; it is real belief. *"Christ"* means "King," and if you really believe in Christ as King, He will rule in your heart. Everybody who really believes in Christ as King makes Christ King. Does Christ sit upon the throne of your heart? Does Christ rule your life? If He does, you are born of God. If He doesn't, you are not.

"Whatsoever is born of God overcometh the world" (1 John 5:4). There are two classes of people in the world: those who are overcoming the world and those who are being overcome by the world. Which class do you belong to? Are you getting the victory over the world, or is the world getting the victory over you? A great many people come to me and say, "I know this is not right, but it is what everybody does in Birmingham, and so I do it." If you could say the same, the world is getting the victory over you! "I don't believe in this, but all the people in our suburb, even including the church members, do it; therefore, I do it." The world is getting the victory over you. If you are born of God, you will get the victory over the

world. You won't ask what the world does; you will ask what Christ says, and you will obey Christ, your King, and get the victory over the world, though you have to stand alone. Are you born of God? *"Ye must be born again."* Have you been born again?

Now, I think, a great many of you will say, "No, I haven't. Can you tell me just now what I must do to be born again?" Yes, I can. God Himself tells us.

*"As many as **received him**, to them gave he power to become the sons of God"* (John 1:12). We are born again by God's Holy Spirit, through His Word, the moment we receive Christ. When you take Christ into your heart, you take the life of God into your heart. When you take Christ into your heart, Christ comes and reigns and transforms you, through and through, in a moment. God, by the power of His Holy Spirit, will make anybody a new creature. I care not how worldly, how sinful, or how hard you are—*anyone* who will throw open his heart and let Jesus come in to rule and reign, who will take Christ as his sin-bearing Savior, his Savior and Deliverer from the power of sin, will be made a new creature.

Some people will bring to you two persons—one who has been very carefully reared, who has been taught to observe the outward forms of Christianity, and another who has gone down into the deepest depths of sin, and say, "This person very near to the kingdom—she will surely be easily led to accept Christ. But we don't expect this person, who has gone down into the depths of sin, to be saved right now." Why not? If that moral, refined, amiable, beautiful girl will take Christ, then God, by His Holy Spirit, will impart His nature to her and make her a child of God the moment she does it. And if the vilest woman will take Christ, then God, by His Holy Spirit, will impart His nature to her, as well, and make her a child of God the moment she does it. How often I have seen it happen at the same meeting.

"*Ye must be born again.*" Ye can be born again. There is not a person reading this book right now who can't become a child of God if he accepts the Lord Jesus Christ. The moment he does it, God, by a creative act, with the power of His Holy Spirit, will make him a new creature. "*Old things are passed away; behold, all things are become new*" (2 Corinthians 5:17).

Two thoughts I wish to leave with you. First, that the most highly educated, upright, amiable, attractive man or woman who is without of Christ will never be saved but by the creative act of God, until the Holy Spirit, in the inmost depths of his or her soul, makes him or her a new creation in Christ. Second, the most hopelessly abandoned man or woman in Birmingham can be saved in an instant, born again, made a new creature, the moment he or she accepts Christ. We are all saved the same way. By the acceptance of Christ, through the power of the Holy Spirit, we are instantly saved. Have you been born again? If not, will you take Jesus right now and be born again?

7

REFUGES OF LIES

"The hail shall sweep away the refuge of lies."
—Isaiah 28:17

Every man needs a refuge from four things: the accusations of his own conscience, the power of sin, the displeasure of God, and the wrath to come. Almost every man has something that he is seeking refuge in. The trouble is not that men have no refuge but that they have a false one, what our text calls a *"refuge of lies."* Just like God announced to Israel through His servant Isaiah, He announces to us today that there is a day coming for testing the refuges of men; and in that day of testing, the hail will sweep away the refuge of lies. Is your refuge in something true or false? Will your refuge stand the test of the times that are coming, or will it go down in the storm? Can we tell? We can, and with absolute certainty!

Four Commonsense Tests

There are four commonsense tests that you can apply to every hope that will show clearly whether it is a true hope or a refuge of lies. First, a true refuge must be one that meets the highest demand of our own conscience. If it does not meet it, it is not a refuge from the accusations of our conscience; neither is it a refuge from the displeasure of God, for if our own heart condemn us, God is greater than our heart and knows all things. (See 1 John 3:20.)

Second, it must be making you a better man. If that refuge in which you are trusting is not making you a better man from day to day, it is not a refuge from the power of sin; neither is it a refuge from the wrath to come, for you may rest assured that any hope that does not save you from the power of sin in the life that now is can never save you from the consequences of sin in the life that is to come.

Third, it must stand the test of the dying hour. A refuge that comforts you only when you are well and strong, failing you in that dread hour when you are face-to-face with death, God, and eternity, is absolutely valueless.

Fourth, it must be a refuge that will stand the test of judgment day. Unless it stands that great test, it is absolutely worthless. Suppose you have a friend who was under indictment for murder, and you go to see him in jail before his trial. You find him in a very cheerful frame of mind, and you say to him, "I thought you were under indictment for murder." And he replies, "I am." "I thought the trial was near." "It is." "Well, you seem to be very cheerful for a man who is under indictment for murder and whose trial is very near." "Oh, I am, and the reason is this: I have an answer to give when the trial comes." "What is your answer? Will it satisfy the judge and jury?" "No, I don't think it will, but it satisfies me." "Why, man," you say, "you don't try the case. Your answer is no good unless it will satisfy the judge and jury." You say you have a refuge that satisfies you. Will it satisfy God? That's the question. On the day of judgment, will it satisfy God?

Commonplace Refuges of Lies

Now I am going to apply these four commonsense tests to some of the refuges of lies in which men are trusting today.

Trust in Our Own Morality, Goodness, and Character

The first refuge of lies is a trust in our own morality, our own goodness, and our own character. How many men and women are there who, when you approach them on the subject of becoming Christians, reply, "No, I don't feel any need of Christ. I am trusting in my own character, in my own daily life. I don't claim to be perfect. Of course, I am not faultless, but I believe that the good in my life will more than counterbalance the evil, and I am trusting in my own good deeds"?

Let us apply the tests. Does your goodness meet the highest demand of your conscience? Be honest, now. In all my talking with moralists, and I have talked with a great many, I have never met in all my life but two men who, when I drove the question home, maintained that their own goodness came up to the highest demand of their own conscience. I have met two. You say that they must have been remarkably good men. No, they had remarkably poor consciences. One of them was a Jew I met in crossing the Atlantic Ocean. I started to talk to him one day about becoming a Christian, and he said to me, "I feel no need of a Savior." I said, "Do you mean to tell me that you have never sinned?" "Never," he said. "Never fallen below the highest demand of your own conscience?" "Never." "Never done anything that you regretted afterward?" "Never." "Well," you say, "he must have been a good man, indeed." No, far from it. He was so mean that before we reached New York City, he was the most unpopular man on the steamer.

Apply the second test. Is trusting in your own goodness making you a better man? As you go on, day after day, talking about your own morality and trusting in it, do you find that, as you grow older, you are growing kinder, humbler, more unselfish, and more considerate? I have known a great many men who have trusted in their own morality; I have never known a single one of them who, as he got older, grew gentler, sweeter, kinder, more considerate of others, and more helpful to his fellow men. All of them grew more cross, censorious, self-centered, and proud.

Apply the third test. Will it stand the test of the dying hour? How often it does not. How many men who have boasted of their own goodness in days of health and strength have wished that they had a living faith in Christ when they come to lie on their dying bed?

In one of my pastorates was perhaps the most self-righteous man I ever knew intimately. He had no use for the church, no use for the Bible, no use for Jesus Christ, no use for ministers, and no use, perhaps least of all, for me, against whom he had a particular grudge because of something I had once done that he misunderstood; but he was perfectly confident that he was the best man in all the community. Over time, cancer appeared on that man's scalp; it spread and ate its way through his scalp until it reached his skull. Then, little by little, it ate away through the skull until there was only a thin film left between the cancer and the brain. You could see his pulse beneath the thin film of skull.

He knew he would die, and in that hour, he said, "Send for Mr. Torrey. I must speak to him." I hurried to his home at once and sat down beside his bed. Then he said to me, "Oh, Mr. Torrey, tell me how to be saved. Tell me how to become a Christian." I took my Bible, and, as simply as I knew how, I explained to him what he must do to be saved—and I think I can explain it pretty simply. But, somehow or other, he could not grasp it. Hour after hour, I sat with him. When night came, I said to his wife and family, "You have sat up with him night after night. You are tired. You go to bed, and I will sit up with him all night tonight and minister to him." They gave me instructions on what to do and retired for the night.

All night long, I sat by him, except for when, now and then, I had to go into the other room to get something for him to eat or drink. Every time I came back into the room where he was lying over in the corner, there came one constant groan from him: "Oh, I wish I was a Christian! Oh, I wish I was a Christian! Oh, I wish I was a Christian!" And so the man died.

Will it stand the test of the judgment day? When you stand face-to-face with God, and that awful, piercing, all-seeing, holy eye looks you through and through—the eye of the One who knows all your past, not only your overt acts, but your covert thoughts, every hidden imagination—will you look up into His face and say, "O God, Thou holy One, Thou all-seeing One, Thou knowest me through and through, and I stand here today confident that my own righteousness will pass with Thee"? Never! If you fancy that you will, get alone with God tonight, kneel down, look up into His face, and try to tell Him that. You can tell me that, but I don't believe that even you have the brazen effrontery to look up into the face of God and tell Him that.

Apply the last test of the Word of God. Will your refuge withstand it? We know that it will not. We are told, *"As many as are of*

the works of the law [who are trying to be saved by their own doings]
*are under the curse: for it is written, Cursed is every one that continu-
eth not in all things which are written in the book of the law to do them"*
(Galatians 3:10). And we are told, *"By the deeds of the law shall no
flesh be justified in his sight"* (Romans 3:20).

Other People's Badness

The second refuge of lies is a trust in other people's badness.
Some people make their boast in their own goodness; others make
their boast in the badness of others. How often, when you go to a
man and urge him to come to Christ, do you receive the reply, "No,
I don't pretend to be very good, but I am just as good as a lot of
other folks, just as good as a great many of your church members"?
Let us try that. Does that meet the highest demand of your own
conscience? When conscience comes with its imperious demands,
does it satisfy your conscience to say, "Well, I am not very good,
but I am as good as somebody else"? If it does, you must have a
mighty mean conscience. Is trust in other people's badness making
you a better man?

I have known a great many people who talked much of other
people's badness, but I have yet to find the first man or woman who
was made better by the process. Show me a man who is always
talking about the faults of others, and I will show you a man who
is rotten at heart every time. Show me a man who calls every other
man a thief, and I will show you a man you can't trust with your
wallet. Show me a man who thinks every other man is impure, and
I will show you an adulterer. Show me a man who is always talking
about others' faults, and I will show you a man, without exception,
whom you can't trust. It never fails.

In my Bible class in one of my pastorates, I had a woman—I
came near saying a lady—who was in business, and was notori-
ously dishonest in business. One day, she said to me in Bible class,

"Brother Torrey"—oh, she did love saying "Brother"—"Brother Torrey, don't you think that everybody in business is dishonest?" I looked at her and replied, "Mrs. Mac—" (she was Scotch; never mind the rest of it), "when anybody in business accuses everybody in business of being dishonest, he convicts at least one person." And she got mad! But why should she have been mad? I told her only the truth.

I made a similar statement in my own church once: "Show me a person who is always talking about the faults of others, and I will show you a person rotten at the heart." At the close, a lady in my church came to me and said, "I didn't like something you said this morning." I replied, "What was that?" "You said, 'Show me a man or woman who is always talking about the faults of others, and I will show you a person rotten at the heart.'" I said, "Yes, I said that, and I meant it, too." "Well," she said, "there is Miss So-and-so, and you must admit she is always talking about the faults of others." I had to admit it. "Now," she said, "you would not say she was bad."

Well, I didn't say it, but the fact was that on that very day, I had told that woman that she could never sing in our choir again, because of some awful rottenness in her life that had been brought to my view—rottenness with which I had charged her and which she had confessed. Men and women, if you know a man or a woman who is always talking about the faults of others, don't trust him or her.

Third, will it stand the test of the dying hour? Oh, never. This very woman to whom I have already referred, who asked the question in the Bible class—the time came for her to die. The physician had done his best. He went into the room and said to her, "Mrs. Mac—, it is my duty to tell you I can do no more; neither can any other physician. You must die." And she shrieked, "Doctor, I can't die! I won't die! I am not ready to die. Doctor, I can't die!" But she did die. And so will you; and in that hour, you will not think about the faults of others—the faults of one person will fill the whole horizon, and those are your own faults.

Will it stand the test of the judgment day? Face-to-face with God who knows you, will you look up into His face and say, "I have never been good, but I am just as good as others"? Never! In that day, God tells us distinctly in Romans 14:12, *"Every one of us shall give account of **himself** to God."*

Universalism

The third refuge of lies is Universalism—the belief that God is too good to condemn anyone, that there is no hell, and that there is no future punishment for sin. How common a refuge that is today, and perhaps no more common anywhere else than in Birmingham. When you urge people to come to Christ, they answer, "I believe in the mercy of God. I believe in the goodness of God. I believe God is love and too good to condemn anyone. I believe there is no hell and no future punishment." Let us apply the tests to this belief.

Does that satisfy the demands of your own conscience? When your conscience points out your sin and demands a change in your life, does it satisfy your conscience to say, "Yes, I know my life is not right, but God is love; therefore, I am going to go right on trampling His laws underfoot, because He is so good and so loving"? Is that the kind of conscience you have? If I had that kind of conscience, I would trade it off as quickly as I could.

Suppose there is a boy who has been very ill. He has a loving mother, who loves him enough to die for him, if necessary. During his long days of illness, she will not even have a hired nurse but stays by his bedside and watches him till she takes his complaint and breaks down. Now he is up and around, but she is on the very verge of death. She calls him and his sister into the room and says,

"Children, I am very low. I may not live till the end of the day, but I want you to go out into the garden into the bright sunshine and enjoy this beautiful day for a while; but, Johnnie, when you get out there, you will find some roses in bloom that are very choice. I am saving them for a special purpose. Please don't pluck them, Johnnie." The children go out, and no sooner do they reach the garden than Johnnie begins at once to pluck every one of those roses. Mary says to him, "Johnnie, what are you doing? Did you not hear what Mother said, that we were not to pull out the roses?" "Oh, yes, Mary, I heard her; but, Mary, you know how Mother loves us. You know how good she is. You know how she watched over me through my illness and how she would not even hire a trained nurse. And now she is ill today because she loved me so and watched over me so tenderly. Mary, that is the reason I am disobeying her, because she loved me so." What would you say of a boy like that?

But some of you are contemptible and ungrateful men and women who are making God's infinite love that gave His Son to die on the cross of Calvary an excuse for trampling His laws underfoot. Shame on you! Don't you ever do that again!

Will Universalism stand the test of the dying hour? A great deal of the Universalism today does not. Dr. Ichabod Spencer, one of the most celebrated pastors America has ever had, has written a book called *Pastoral Sketches*, in which he shares incidents from his pastoral work. It is one of the most valuable books that a minister can possess. One sketch is as follows: Two of his Brooklyn congregants, a married woman and her mother-in-law, were both married to non-Christians. One day, the husband of the younger—the son of the older—was taken suddenly and seriously ill. His wife and mother saw that the illness might result in death, and so they sent for Dr. Ichabod Spencer.

When Dr. Spencer came into the room, this young fellow was tossing with sickness upon a bed. Dr. Spencer hurried to his side and tried to present to him the consolation of the gospel. But the man replied, "Dr. Spencer, I can't listen to you. I have heard it over and over again. I would not listen to it in times of health and strength. I am now very ill. I am dying and will die soon. I can't repent in this, my last hour. I can't do it." And he tossed and groaned in agony upon the bed. His father was walking back and forth in the room in great agitation. Finally, he turned to the bed and said, "My son, there is nothing for you to be so anxious about. You have not been a bad boy, and there is no hell. You have nothing to fear." That dying son turned to his father and said, "Father, you have deceived me all through my life. If I had listened to Mother instead of to you, I would not be here now. She tried to get me to go to church and Sunday school, but you took me off fishing and pleasure-seeking on the Sabbath. You told me that there was no hell, and I believed you. You have deceived me up to this time, but, Father, you can't deceive me any longer. I am dying and going to hell, and my blood is upon your soul." Then he turned his face to the wall and died. Fathers, you who are upsetting the teaching of godly wives—the day is coming when your sons will curse you. Will your Universalism stand the test of the dying hour?

Is it making you a better man? Much of today's Universalism doesn't. Oh, to so many, Universalism is simply an excuse for sin! The world is sweeping in like a flood in so many of our churches today. All separation is gone, and professed Christians are running after the world, the flesh, and the devil, because they have accepted the nonsense that is robbing the church of its devotion and its beauty, and making the church so much like the world that you can't tell the two apart. This Universalistic nonsense is simply an excuse for sin—to make men comfortable in a life of sin and of giving up their separation to God. Face it squarely—is your Universalism making you a better person?

Again, will it stand the test of the judgment day? When you go up to meet God face-to-face, will you look into His face and say, "O God, I know my life has not been right, but I thought that Thou were a God of love. I thought that Thou were too good to punish sin. I did not think there was any hell, so I trampled Thy laws underfoot"? Would you say that? You know you wouldn't.

Infidelity

The next refuge of lies is infidelity. Many men are trying to find comfort tonight in infidelity. Let us apply the tests. Does your infidelity meet the highest demand of your own conscience? When conscience points out your sin and demands a new life, does it satisfy your conscience to say, "Well, I don't believe in the Bible, and I don't believe in God. I don't believe that Jesus Christ is the Son of God"? Does that satisfy your conscience? If it does, you are not fit to be called a human being.

Is your infidelity making you a better man? I have known a great many infidels. My ministry has been largely a ministry to skeptics, agnostics, and infidels. I have had their confidence, and I have yet to meet the first infidel who was made better by infidelity. I have known men—countless men—whose characters have been undermined by infidelity. Oh, I have had young men come to me with breaking hearts, with sad confessions of immorality and of ruin, and I have had them say to me time and again, "The first step was listening to Colonel Ingersoll," or some other infidel lecturer, or reading an infidel book.

I tell you men—young men, especially—who are trifling with infidelity: You are undermining the foundations of sound character. Infidelity is sowing the world with wickedness. One night in my own church in Chicago, to which a good many infidels come, one man said to me, "We come over here to hear you. You don't spare us, but we like men to stand up to the rack. That is the reason we come." There are always a lot of them every Sunday. Thank God, a great many of them get converted, so we like to see them coming. They are very friendly and very kind. When we left Chicago, I think the person who came nearest to breaking into tears was the wife of one of the most notorious infidels in Chicago. She was an infidel herself, or trying to be. But now for my story.

One night in my church in Chicago, I said, "I would like to put this thing to the test. I would like to ask every man in this congregation tonight who has been saved from drunkenness by Jesus Christ and the Bible to stand up." And all over that building, about two hundred men stood up as having been saved from drunkenness by the Bible and Christ. I said, "That will do. Now I am going to be fair. I would like to ask every man in this audience who has been saved from drunkenness or any other definite sin by infidelity in any form to stand up." I thought that no one had risen, but finally, as I looked over that great crowd, way off underneath the gallery, I saw one man standing—a poor, seedy-looking fellow—the only man in the audience who had been saved from drunkenness or other positive sin by infidelity; and he was drunk at the time. But he had sense enough to come to Christ at the close of the meeting. Men, face facts. Infidelity makes nobody a better man.

Will it stand the test of the dying hour? How often it fails. A friend of mine who was in the Union Army in the Civil War said that in the same company with him was a man who was a very outspoken infidel. He talked much in the camp. On the second day of the battle of Pittsburg Landing, he said to the boys in the morning,

"Boys, it just seems as if I am going to be shot today." "Oh," they said, "nonsense. It is nothing but superstition. You are not going to be shot." "Well," he said, "I feel very strange. I feel as if I am going to be shot."

At last, they were lined up, waiting for the word of command. Upon hearing "Forward, march!" up they went, climbing the hill; and just as they reached the crest, a volley came from the enemy's guns. At the very first volley, a bullet pierced the man near his heart, and as he fell back into the arms of his comrade, he threw his hands up in the air and cried out, "O God, just give me time to repent." It took only one bullet to take the infidelity out of that man. It would take less than that to take the nonsense out of most of you.

Will it stand the test of the judgment day? Will you enter God's presence and be ready to say, "O God, my answer is this: I was an infidel, I was an agnostic, I was a skeptic, I was an atheist, I was a materialist, I was a positivist," or this, that, and the other? Do you think you will? I will tell you how to put it to the test. Get alone tonight, kneel down, and try to tell Him. Oh, you can talk nonsense to your fellow men. But when you go to talk to God, it will take the nonsense out of you. One night, I went down into the audience to speak to individuals after a meeting like this. I went down to a man who sat in the last opera chair. I said to him, "Are you a Christian?" "No," he said, "I should say not. I am an infidel." I said, "What do you mean?" "Well," he said, "I don't believe in the divinity of Christ." I said, "You don't believe in the divinity of Christ?" "No," he said, "I don't." "Well," I said, "let us kneel down right now and tell God so." And he turned pale. You go and tell God what you would like to tell me.

Religion

One more refuge of lies is religion. You say, "What! Religion? You don't mean what you say." I mean every word. I say religion is just as much a refuge of lies as morality, other people's bad-ness, Universalism, and infidelity. Religion never saved anybody. It is one thing to trust in religion; it is something entirely dif-ferent to trust in the living Christ. How many men are boasting in their religion? They go to people and say, "Oh, I am very reli-gious. I go to church. I say my prayers every morning and night. I read my Bible. I go to Communion. I have been baptized. I have been confirmed. I give a tenth of my income to the poor. I am very religious." Well, you can do every bit of that and go straight to hell.

Others say, "I make my confession on Saturday and attend mass on Sunday. I say ever so many Paternosters and Ave Marias. I count my beads and sprinkle myself with holy water." You can do it all and go straight to hell. Religion never saved anybody.

Apply the tests. Is your religion making you a better man or woman? A great deal of religion doesn't make men or women a bit better. There are some people who say prayers, read the Bible, go to church, talk in meetings, and are very prominent in the church who will lie as fast as anybody else. Many people who do all these things will go around slandering their neighbors. Many men who are very religious and very prominent in the church—I don't know whether it is so in your town or not, for I don't know your town—will cut people wide open in a business deal, as any other man in town would do. Many religious men treat their servants like brutes and oppress their employees. Many religious men turn a deaf ear to the cry of the widow and the orphan, unless it is going to get them in the papers. Many religious men are perfect scoundrels.

One Sabbath morning, I met a man who seemed to be a most religious man. He said to me, "I am going to conduct a meeting." He had dressed to make himself look as much like a preacher as he could. He made his employees gather together at a certain hour every day for prayer, and he held religious service with them every Sunday so that they would not have to go to church. Someone told me that this pious humbug was paying starvation wages to the girls who worked for him. I saw the girls, and they were the palest, most pinched crowd of girls I have seen in all of England; and man after man told me of how he tried to get the better of them in deals. That kind of religion will send a man to the deepest hell there is.

In the second place, will your religion stand the test of the dying hour? A great deal of religion doesn't. A great many very actively religious people are as badly scared as anybody else when they come to die. Oh, how I have heard them groan and sigh and weep in the dying hour. Their hollow religion doesn't stand the test of that great crisis.

Will it stand the test of the judgment day? Mere religion will not, for the Lord Jesus Christ Himself said, *"Many will say to me in that day, Lord, Lord, have we not prophesied in thy name? and in thy name have cast out devils? and in thy name done many wonderful works? And then will I profess unto them, I never knew you: depart from me, ye that work iniquity"* (Matthew 7:22–23). Religion is a refuge of lies, and if that is what you are trusting in, you are lost forever unless you get something better.

True Refuge

"Well," someone will ask, "is there a true refuge?" There is. God said, *"Behold, I lay in Zion for a foundation a stone, a tried stone, a precious corner stone, a sure foundation: he that believeth shall not make haste"* (Isaiah 28:16). That sure foundation stone is Jesus Christ. *"Other foundation can no man lay than that which is laid, which is Jesus Christ"* (1 Corinthians 3:11).

I said a few moments ago that it is one thing to trust in religion and something entirely different to trust in a crucified and risen

Christ with a living faith. Will that refuge stand the test of our own conscience? It will, thank God. When my conscience points to my sin, I have an answer that satisfies it, and that answer is "Jesus," who bore my sins in His own body on the cross.

Will it make men better men? Yes. A living faith in a crucified and living Christ will make every man who has it more and more like Christ every day of his life. And if you have a faith that is not making you like Christ, you have not a real faith. Whosoever believeth that Jesus is the Son of God overcomes the world. (See 1 John 5:4–5.) If the world is overcoming you, you do not have a living, saving faith in the Son of God.

Will it stand the test of the dying hour? Thank God, yes. How often have I gone to dying beds and looked men and women and children, too, in the face and said to them, "My brother/my sister, your time is short. Before morning breaks, you will have passed into the great beyond," and with a calm, triumphant, ecstatic voice, they said, "I know it; I am ready to go."

The gladdest scenes I have ever seen on earth have been deathbed scenes of true Christians—scenes of triumph and glory. One day, at the close of my Bible class in Chicago, the president of the class came up to me and said, "Pomeroy"—one of the members of my class—"is dying round the corner of consumption. I don't think he will live until morning. I know you are busy, but can you go and see him?" I said, "Certainly, Fred." I went around and found him propped up with pillows. I said to him, "Mr. Pomeroy, they tell me you can't live through the night." "Oh," he said, "I know it." I said, "Are you afraid to die?" "Afraid?" he said. "Afraid to die? No, I shall be glad to depart and be with Christ." How often I have seen it.

Will it stand the test of the judgment day? Yes. If it is God's will—I say it reverently and thoughtfully—if it is God's will, I am willing to face God tonight in judgment. You say, "What, have you never sinned?" Alas! I have. Thank God, you will never know how deeply I have sinned. But when God asks for an answer, I will say one word—*Jesus*—and that will satisfy God. It already satisfies me.

Men and women, the hail shall sweep away every refuge of lies. Throw them all away tonight and come to Christ, so you are ready for life, ready for death, and ready for eternity.

8

FOUND OUT

"Be sure your sin will find you out."
—Numbers 32:23

No man can escape his own sins. Every sin we commit will find us and call us to account and make us pay. No man ever committed a single sin that he did not pay for in some way. No man ever committed a single sin by which he was not a loser. The most stupendous folly of which a man can be guilty is for him to imagine that he can ever gain anything by doing wrong. Whether you hurt anyone else by your own wrongdoing or not, you are bound to hurt yourself. Doubtless, there are many men and women reading this who contemplate doing some wrong act. Very likely you contemplate doing it today. I want to say to you, as Moses said to the children of Reuben and Gad, *"Be sure your sin will find you out"* (Numbers 32:23). You can't escape it. You are bound to suffer by that sin. It is pretty sure that if a man puts his hand in the fire, he will be burned. It is absolutely certain that if a man sins, he will suffer for it, along with each individual sin he commits. You may escape the law, but you cannot escape the consequences of your own sins. You may escape the laws of men, but you cannot escape the law of God. No man can hide from his sins. He will be found out. Let me point out some ways in which a man's sins find him out.

Execution of Human Laws

Men's sins find them out by the execution of human laws. The execution of the law in human society is necessarily imperfect, and yet it is astonishing how surely men who break the law are sooner or later brought to book. A man may successfully elude the meshes of the law for days or weeks or months or years, but he is all the time weaving a net that will almost certainly entrap him at last.

Take an illustration. Some years ago, a crime was committed in the city of Chicago. The detectives set to work to ferret out the criminal. Every clue failed. One day, a detective was speaking to me about it. He was utterly discouraged. We were just about to separate when, at the last moment, a thought flashed through my mind about a man who had not been suspected. That man had thought he'd covered all his tracks and that not a soul on earth but himself knew that he was the criminal. But within two hours, he was under arrest and had made full confession of his crime. It is a marvelous thing how crime comes to light, how a man's sin finds him out and exposes him at last to the contempt of the whole world.

Harm to the Body

Furthermore, men's sins find them out in their own bodies. When a man does not pay the penalty of his sin before human courts, he pays it in a court where there is no possibility of brib-ery—the court of physical retribution for moral offenses. Not only do certain diseases follow in the train of certain sins, but, in a general way, there is an intimate connection between morality and health. All sins have physical consequences. The suffering con-sequent upon some sins is not as immediate or as marked as the physical suffering consequent upon a few well-known vices, but it is nonetheless true that every sin has physical consequences. The man who sins will suffer for it in his body. His sin is bound to find him out.

Scarcely a week passes that someone does not come to me suf-fering some great physical evil that is simply the consequence of his own sin. Young men see others suffering the terrible consequences of transgressing God's law, yet they go right on sinning, as oxen to the slaughter. They fancy that they will be an exception, but there are no exceptions to physical law. Any action that is unnatural or immoral is bound to be visited with penalty.

Why are there so many men with broken bodies and shattered intellects? Violation of God's law—their sin has found them out. Why so many broken-down women? Violation of God's law—their sin has found them out. Of course, disease may be hereditary, or the result of accident or misfortune; but if we should eliminate all the sickness that is the direct or indirect result of our own sin, we would be surprised at the little sickness there would be left. Many very excellent young men have been guilty of sins in cer-tain directions, and the body is shattered and the mind enfeebled in consequence. The same is true of many young women, who, in many other respects, are most estimable young women. Take as the sin of anger. Does that find a man out in his body? Surely. It disorders his blood, stomach, brain, and nerves. It is demonstrably unhealthy in every case, and in many cases, it leads to paralysis and death.

In one church I pastored, one of the deacons had a stroke that finally resulted in death. It was said that the stroke this excellent man suffered was due to losing his temper in a political discussion. It is simply marvelous, if you will only study it, the many ways—some simple, some intricate, some direct, and some indirect—in which our sins hunt us down and find us out in our own bodies. Man, if you are contemplating sin, just stop and think of this a moment: *"Be sure your sin will find you out"*! If it finds you out nowhere else, it will in that body of yours. For every sin you commit, you will in some measure pay a physical penalty.

Personal Character

There is another place in which our sin finds us out, one that is, by far, more important than its finding us out by the execution of human laws or in our bodies. Sin finds us out in our character. For every sin you commit, your character will suffer. Every sin breeds a moral ulcer. A festering character is worse than a festering body. You can't tell a lie without your moral blood being poisoned by it and your moral constitution being undermined. Do you think you can cheat a man in business and not suffer in your character more than he suffers in his pocket? Do you think that you can wrong an employee in his wages and not suffer immeasurably more in what you become than he suffers in what he gets? Do you think you can wrong a man regarding his wife and not develop a death-dealing cancer in your own character? Do you think you can read an impure book or tell or listen to an obscene story and not breed a stinking distemper in your own moral nature? Do you think you can violate the laws of purity that God has written in His Word, on your heart, and in your body, and not reap disgusting tumors in your own character? Wherever else the law may seem to fail, here it absolutely never fails. Man's sin always finds him out in his character, in what he himself becomes.

Conscience

Again, your sin will find you out in your own conscience. You may be able to hide your sin from everyone, but you cannot hide it from yourself. And you are so constricted in the mercy of God that to know you are a sinner means self-condemnation and agony. Oh, how many of you are suffering untold agonies from the bitter consciousness of sins no one but yourself knows anything about. No physical torments match the torments of an accusing conscience. An accusing conscience means hell on earth. No earthly prosperity, human love, mirth, music, revelry, fun, or intoxication can dispel its clouds or assuage the agony of its ever-gnawing tooth. Well did the old Latin poet Juvenal write:

> Trust me, nor tortures that the poets feign
> Can match the fierce, the unutterable pain
> He feels, who, night and day, devoid of rest,
> Carries his own accuser in his breast.

Ah! There is a place where all our sins will find us out—every one of us. Have no doubt of that, my friend. *"Be sure your sin will find you out."* It may be hidden from the officer of the law; it may be hidden from the eye of every man and every woman; but it will speak to your conscience some day. It will find you there, then beware! That sin you are contemplating looks fair and sweet. But it won't look so fair and sweet after it is committed. It will find you out, and you will suffer. Oh, how you will suffer.

Before I pass on to another place where sin will find you out, let me say that the fact that your sin is sure to find you out in so many ways—in your relations to your fellow men, in your body, in your character, and in your conscience—all this points unmistakably to the existence of a moral governor of this universe. Everything in this universe is tuned to virtue. The stars in their courses fight against Sisera. (See Judges 5:20.) Everything conspires to punish sin and reward goodness. To see this and to question the existence of such a God as the Bible pictures is to be supremely irrational.

Children

Another way your sin will find you out is through your children. That is one of the most awful things about sin—its curse falls not only upon us but upon our children, as well. God does visit the iniquities of the fathers upon the children. (See, for example, Exodus 20:5.) You may complain about that as much as you like, but it is an unquestionable fact; and a wise man doesn't think as much of what he would like to have true as of what really is true. There is no question that our sins find us out through our children.

For example, a drinking man may not be a very hard drinker, but his habit will almost certainly be a curse upon his children. It is more than likely that one of his sons will be a drunkard. I remember a man who was a constant but moderate drinker. I don't think that man was ever drunk in his life; indeed, he despised drunkards, but he laughed at total abstainers. Each one of his three sons became a drunkard later in life.

In a New England town, I knew of a young woman belonging to one of the best families. I don't think that her father was a drunkard, only a moderate drinker, but the daughter inherited an appetite that completely overmastered her. She became a periodical drunkard. At times, she would disappear from home and go to Boston. One time, she was found beastly drunk in the lowest slums. Her father's sin had found him out.

Take the liquor dealer. His sin is almost sure to find him out in his children. A friend of mine of very wide experience says he never has known a man in the liquor business where the curse did not sooner or later strike in his own home. A man was pointed out to me in an American town as the one who had made a determined effort to upset the temperance principles of the majority of the town by introducing a saloon. Two members of his own family came to violent deaths through drink. His sin found him out.

Take the Sabbath breaker. Nowadays, a great many Christians are careless about the Lord's Day. They go out riding or to the park or bicycling or to play golf. Let them look out, for their sin will find them out through their children. Their children will go further than they do. They will disregard the day altogether. They will very likely turn out to be infidels and drunkards and rakes and all that is bad. If there is one thing I thank God for in my home training, it is the strictness with which we children were trained to observe the Lord's Day. Some of us wandered into sin later on in life, but when that one day in seven came around, we couldn't find the heart to do what we did on other days. We would go to church, and so we were brought back to Christ.

The sin of the adulterer will find him out in his own children. Let him take heed regarding his daughter. A very prominent man in America, an excellent man in many respects, was led on into sin. Very few knew of it. His wife knew of it and freely forgave him. But his sin found him out in his own family. His own daughter fell prey to an infamous scoundrel. Oh, men and women who are contemplating some sinful act: Beware, lest you bring a curse upon your own household. It looks attractive today; it seems as if it would pay, but it won't. *"Be sure your sin will find you out."*

Eternity

Last, your sin will find you out in eternity. This present life is not the end. There is a future life, and our acts and their consequences will follow us into it. If your sin does not find you out here, it will there. You may be absolutely sure of that. In eternity, we shall reap the consequences of every sin we sowed in time. It sometimes seems to go on here to the end, unwhipped of justice. Men defraud their employees, rob the widow and the orphan, and condemn other men and their families to beggary, that they may increase their already too enormous wealth; and no one seems to call them to account. It will not always be so. God will call them to account—to strict account—and a few thousand, or hundreds of thousands or millions, of their ill-gotten wealth given to charity will not blind the eyes of a holy God. They shall suffer.

Men sometimes lay traps for foolish girls, and they go down to ruin and contempt and an outcast's grave, and it seems that no one calls them to account. They go on and on, are admitted to the "best society," and are loaded with honors. It will not always be so. Their sin will find them out—if not in this world, then in the next. And they will stand before the universe exposed to shame, loaded with dishonor, and cast out to everlasting contempt.

Men despise God, laugh at His Word, and trample underfoot His Son; and God still lets them live. He does not seem to call them to account. But it will not be always so.

> *The Lord Jesus shall be revealed from heaven with his mighty angels, in flaming fire taking vengeance on them that know not God, and that obey not the gospel of our Lord Jesus Christ: who shall be punished with everlasting destruction from the presence of the Lord, and from the glory of his power.*
>
> (2 Thessalonians 1:7–9)

"*Be sure your sin will find you out.*" The principle of our text is sure. All history is a confirmation of and commentary on this point of the Word of God. Every man's experience is a confirmation of it. You cannot sin without suffering for it. Your sin will find you out in the workings of human society, in your own body, in your character, in your conscience, in your children, in eternity, or in all of these together. Are you a man or woman contemplating sin right now? Don't do it. I beg of you, don't do it. You will regret it. You will suffer, and you will pay an awful price. Your sin will find you out.

But many of us have sinned already, and our sins are finding us out already. What shall we do? Fly to Christ. I have preached law to you. Now, a word of gospel. There is but one way of escape from the penalties of the law, and that is in the grace of the gospel. *"Christ hath redeemed us from the curse of the law, being made a curse for us"* (Galatians 3:13). Fly to Him at once. He calls, *"Come unto Me, all ye that labor and are heavy laden, and I will give you rest"* (Matthew 11:28). Come—come at once.

9

"WHO THEN CAN BE SAVED?"

"Who then can be saved?"
—Mark 10:26

The disciples asked that question of Jesus. He had just told them how hard it was for a rich man to enter into the kingdom of heaven, and it seems the disciples held the same opinion as most men hold today, that a rich man can get anywhere. But Jesus said no; it was easier for a camel to pass through the eye of a needle than for a rich man to enter the kingdom of God. Then they asked the question "If that is so—if it is so hard for a rich man to be saved—what chance does anybody else stand?"

"Who then can be saved?" Jesus went on to tell them that though it was impossible for a rich man to be saved—and I think all experience attests to this, that the rich man stands the poorest chance

of salvation of anybody on earth—God, with whom all things are possible (see Matthew 19:26; Mark 10:27), could save even a rich man—but He alone could do so.

We come, then, to the question "*Who then can be saved?*" The Bible answers the question very fully and very plainly. It tells us that there are some people who cannot be saved and that there are some people who can be saved.

Who Cannot Be Saved?

First, we will take up those who cannot be saved.

He Who Will Not Give Up His Sin

First, no man can be saved who will not give up his sin. We read, "*Let the wicked forsake his way, and the unrighteous man his thoughts: and let him return unto the Lord, and he will have mercy upon him; and to our God, for he will abundantly pardon*" (Isaiah 55:7). But if he will not forsake his ways and turn to God, he cannot be saved.

Every man and every woman has to choose between sin and salvation. You cannot have both. If you won't give up sin, you must give up salvation. In our day, there are schemes of salvation that propose to save a man while he continues in his sin, but these are absurdities upon the very face. We read in Matthew 1:21, concerning our Savior, "*Thou shalt call his name Jesus: for he shall save his people from their sins.*" Not *in* them but *from* them. You cannot save a man while he continues in sin. Sin is damnation; holiness is salvation. And you might just as well propose to cure a man who is ill while he continues in his disease as save a sinner while he continues in his sin. A man is not cured till he is well, and a man is not saved till he quits his sin.

The whole reason why some of you are not saved is because you won't give up your sin. Some of you won't give up your drunkenness; some of you won't give up your adultery; some of you won't give up your profanity; some of you won't give up your lying; some of you won't give up your bad temper; some won't give up one thing, and some won't give up another. Well then, you must go into perdition. You cannot be saved if you won't give up sin; and if you persist in sinning, you will be lost forever.

A man in Chicago came to a friend of mine and said to him, "I want to be saved." My friend replied, "You do not want to be saved." "But," he said, "I do." My friend said, "You are not willing to give up your drinking." "No," he said, "I am not." He answered, "Well then, you do not want to be saved. To be saved means to give up sin." Jesus Christ can save any man; but He won't and can't save a man who won't give up his sin.

He Who Trusts in His Own Righteousness

Second, no man can be saved who trusts in his own righteousness and is not willing to admit that he is a lost sinner. That is the trouble with hundreds of people—they are proud of their own morality and are not willing to get down to the dust and say, "I am a poor, vile, worthless, miserable sinner." These people will never be saved, and never can be saved, because they trust in their own righteousness.

In the eighteenth chapter of Luke, Jesus tells us that two men went up to the temple to pray. The one was a Pharisee—one of the most respectable, religious men in the community, whom everybody looked up to; the other was a publican, a man whom everybody looked down upon. When the Pharisee prayed, he talked about his own goodness. He looked up and said, *"I thank thee, that I am not as other men are, extortioners, unjust, adulterers"* (Luke 18:11). Then he looked contemptuously over to the poor publican and said, *"Or even as this publican. I fast twice in the week, I give tithes of all that I possess"* (Luke 18:11–12). Pretty religious, wasn't he? And Jesus said that this man went out of the temple and down to his house as an unforgiven, hopelessly lost sinner; but the publican—the outcast, the man that everybody looked down upon—would not so much as lift up his eyes to heaven but felt he was a miserable, worthless sinner. He smote upon his breast and said, *"God be merciful to me a sinner"* (Luke 18:13). And Jesus said that this man went down to his house justified. Anybody can be saved who will take the sinner's place and cry for mercy; nobody else can.

I have a very quaint American friend who is a Scotchman, and one day he was walking through the country when a man came along in a carriage. He saw the old man walking and invited him to get into the carriage, which he very promptly accepted, for he saw an opportunity for doing good. The driver was very curious to know who the old Scotchman was, so he asked him some questions, and finally the old Scotchman said, "I will tell you who I am, and I will tell you what my business is. I have a very strange business: I am hunting for heirs." The other man said, "What?" "I am hunting for heirs—heirs to a great estate. I represent a very great estate, and I am hunting for heirs for it, and there are a good many round this neighborhood." The other said, "Do you mind telling me their names?" "No," he said. "It is a very large family; their name begins with *s*." "Oh," said the man, "Smith, I suppose?" "No," the old man replied, "a much larger family than the Smith family." The other replied, "Larger than the Smith family! Who are they?" The old Scotchman said, "They are the sinner family. The estate I represent is the kingdom of God, the inheritance incorruptible and undefiled, that fadeth not away. The heirs to it are the sinners who are willing to take the family name and own up to the fact that they are sinners and look to God for pardon."

Do you belong to the sinner family? If you do, you can be saved. If you are not willing to own that you do, you cannot be saved. You will be lost forever.

He Who Is Not Willing to Accept the Free Gift of Salvation

Third, no man or woman who is not willing to accept salvation as a free gift can be saved. Scripture says, *"For by grace are ye saved through faith; and that not of yourselves: it is the gift of God"* (Ephesians 2:8), and *"The gift of God is eternal life through Jesus Christ our Lord"* (Romans 6:23). Salvation is a free gift. Anybody can have it for nothing; nobody can have it any other way; and if you are not willing to take it as a free gift, you cannot have it at all.

One day, my wife was talking to the son of the richest man in a particular neighborhood in America. There seemed to be some difficulty about his accepting Christ. Finally, my wife called him by his name and said to him, "The trouble with you is, you are not willing to accept salvation as a free gift." He said, "Mrs. Torrey, that is just it—I am not willing to accept salvation as a free gift. If I could earn it, if I could work for it, if I could deserve it, I am willing to earn it; but I am not willing to take it as a free gift."

Well, nobody can earn it, nobody can merit it, and nobody can deserve it; nobody can get it except for nothing, and unless you are willing to take it as a free gift, you will never get it at all. The richest millionaire has to get it the same way as the poorest pauper—as a free gift. And the richest saved man on earth will have nothing more to boast of when he gets to heaven than the poorest saved pauper.

He Who Will Not Accept Jesus Christ as Savior

Fourth, nobody can be saved who will not accept Jesus Christ as his Savior. We are told in Acts 4:12, *"There is none other name under heaven given among men, whereby we must be saved."* Anybody can be saved in Christ; nobody can be saved any other way. An infidel once said to my friend Mr. Henry Varley, "If I cannot be saved without accepting Christ, I won't be saved." Well then, he won't be saved. That is all there is to it—he won't be saved.

If you ever go to Sydney, you will soon find that every citizen in the city is very proud of his harbor. You won't be in Sydney half an hour before somebody asks you what you think of his harbor. He may well be proud of it, for it is one of the finest harbors, if not the finest harbor, in the world, beautiful and capacious. But it has only one entrance. There is one high promontory of rock called North Head and another high promontory called South Head, and the only channel, wide and deep, is between these two heads. A little way south of South Head is another headland called "Jacob's Ladder."

One night many years ago, a vessel called the *Duncan Dunbar*, with hundreds of people on board, sailed outside of Sydney harbor after dark. The captain saw South Head and mistook it for North Head; he saw "Jacob's Ladder" and mistook it for South Head. He steered the vessel full speed ahead in between the two lights and ran onto the rocks. Every one of the hundreds on board perished, except for one man, who was thrown up into a cave on the face of the rock. Now, that captain was perfectly sincere—there never was a sincerer man on earth—but he was mistaken, and he was lost. People say it does not make a difference what you believe if you are sincere; but the more sincerely you believe error, the worse off you are. There is just one channel into salvation, and that is Christ. Try to go any other way, and no matter how sincere you are, you will be wrecked and lost eternally.

Who Can Be Saved?

Now that we talked about who cannot be saved, we will discuss who can be saved.

The Vilest Sinner

First, sinners can be saved, even the vilest. Paul wrote, *"This is a faithful saying, and worthy of all acceptation, that Christ Jesus came into the world to save sinners; of whom I am chief"* (1 Timothy 1:15). Jesus Christ has already saved the chief of sinners, and He is able to do it again.

In Minneapolis, where I used to live, a girl of thirteen was betrayed by her family. Her father and mother cast her off, so much the more shame for them. Her brothers cast her off, and I doubt if they were any better than she; but, you know, it is one thing for a girl to sin and another thing for a man to sin. It is in the eyes of man, but it is not in the eyes of God. They cast off this poor thirteen-year-old, and I think they were worse than she was—more devilish.

Of course, she went down; she became the companion of thieves, robbers, forgers, murderers, and everything that was disreputable. She was a member of two of the worst gangs in New York and Chicago. One night, a friend of mine met her and said to her, "If you are ever sick of this life, come to me, and I will help you out of it."

A night came when she was thoroughly sick of her life, and she went to the house of this gentleman, who was very wealthy and used all his money for God—pretty much all of it. His wife, who was in, tried to show this young woman the way of life. After a while, the gentleman came in and showed her the way of life, and she was saved. Today, that young woman occupies a high position of great responsibility and honor in America, and there is scarcely one in society who knows of her past life. God has covered it up, though she bears the same name she had in her former life.

A few years ago, when I was in Northfield, she came to me and said, "I hope, Mr. Torrey, that you and Mrs. Torrey won't think it necessary to tell the people here my story," for we were about the only ones there who knew her past record; she had been in our house in the days of her trouble. I said, "Most assuredly, we shall not," for why should you tell a saved woman's story when it is underneath the blood, any more than a saved man's story? It is no longer her story; it is blotted out. And today, that woman is a highly honored woman. Out of the deepest depth of sin, Jesus Christ has not only saved her but also covered up her past.

He Who Is Too Weak to Resist Sin in His Own Strength

Second, anyone who is too weak to resist sin in his own strength can be saved. It is not a question of your strength but of Christ's strength. We read in Jude 24–25, "*Now unto him that is able to keep you from falling, and to present you faultless before the presence of his glory with exceeding joy, to the only wise God our Savior, be glory and majesty.*" We read in 1 Peter 1:5, "*Who are kept by the power of God through faith unto salvation.*" Jesus Christ can keep the weakest man or woman just as well as the strongest.

I have seen men start out in the Christian life who talk this way in testimony meetings: "Friends, you know me; I am a man of great decision of character. When I make up my mind to do anything, I always go through. I have started out in this Christian life, and I want you to understand that I am not going to backslide as so many do; I am going through." Whenever I hear a man talking that way, I know he is going to backslide within six weeks every time. Another man will stand up, trembling and hesitant, and will say, "You all know me; you know I have no willpower left. I have tried to quit my sin, time and time again, and, as you know, I have failed every time. I have absolutely no confidence in myself; but God says in Isaiah 41:10, '*Fear thou not; for I am with thee: be not* dismayed; for I am thy God: I will strengthen thee; yea, I will help thee; yea, I will uphold thee with the right hand of my righteousness,' and I am trusting in Him." When I hear a man talking that way, I know he is going to stand every time.

One day in Chicago, somebody came up to me and said, "We have got to find a place for Mrs. S—."

I asked, "Why?"

"Well," he replied, "Nels got drunk last night and tried to kill his wife with a shoe knife, and it is not safe for her or her child to be around her husband, so she left. We must do something to provide for her."

I said, "You are quite right to provide for her; that is just what we ought to do."

Not long after, Nels came round to me and said, "Mr. Torrey, do you know where my wife is?"

"I do."

"Will you please tell me where she is?"

I replied, "I will not. You tried to kill her. You are a brute. You do not deserve to have a wife, and I am not going to tell you where she is, to let you go and kill her."

He insisted, "If you do not tell me, I will commit suicide."

"Very well," I said. "You will go to hell if you do."

That kind of fellow never commits suicide. Well, he kept getting drunk. He could not help it, poor fellow. Every little while, he would come round to me for five cents, or ten cents, saying that he was going to get a job in a shoe factory. I always knew that the money was going for whiskey. He got a good many five-cent pieces from me, and a good many from my students, and the money always went for whiskey.

Years and years went on, and Nels was always saying that he was going to quit drinking. I knew he was not. He meant to. He would come round, saying that he was hunting for work; but I knew he was looking for another drink. That went on for years. One day, I said to God, "Heavenly Father, if You will give me Nels S—, I will never despair of another man as long as I live." I do not know if it was the same week, but I am sure it was very soon afterward, that Nels S— set his feet upon the Rock, Christ Jesus, and never fell again. Years have passed, and he is an honored member of my church. When I was home this summer, among those who came to welcome me was Nels S—, his wife, and his child, a happy family in Jesus Christ.

Friends, the Christ who saved Nels S—, the lying, habitual, hopeless drunkard, can save any man or woman who will trust Him.

He Who Has Committed the Unpardonable Sin but Is Willing to Come to Christ

Once more, any man can be saved who thinks he has committed the unpardonable sin, if he is willing to come to Jesus Christ. Jesus says in John 6:37, "*Him that cometh to me I will in no wise cast out.*" I think I have never gone to any place in my life where somebody has not written to me or come to me and said, "I have committed the unpardonable sin," and almost every one of them has gone away rejoicing in Jesus Christ. Every week, I get letters from people all over England who tell me that they have committed the unpardonable sin.

One time, I received a letter from a brokenhearted Presbyterian minister. He wrote that he had a son who was in awful spiritual darkness. The son thought that he had committed the unpardonable sin, and he was plunged into absolute despair. The father wanted to know if I would take him at the Bible institute. I told him that although I had every sympathy with him in his sorrow, the Bible institute was not for the purpose of helping cases like these but rather to train men and women for Christian service.

The father continued writing to me, beseeching me to take his son, and he got other friends to plead for him. Finally, I consented to take the young man. He was sent to me under guard, lest he do some rash thing by the way.

When he was brought to my office, I showed him to a seat. As soon as the others had left the room, he began the conversation by saying, "I am possessed of the devil."

"I think quite likely you are," I replied, "but Christ is able to cast out devils."

"You do not understand me," he interjected. "I mean that the devil has entered into me as he did into Judas Iscariot."

"That may be," I answered, "but Christ came to destroy the works of the devil. Now He says in John 6:37, *'Him that cometh to me I will in no wise cast out.'* If you will just come to Him, He will receive you and set you free from Satan's power."

The conversation went on in this way for some time: he constantly asserting the absolute hopelessness of his case, and I constantly asserting the power of Jesus Christ and His promise, *"Him that cometh to me I will in no wise cast out."* After a while, I sent the young man to his room. Days and weeks passed, and we had many conversations, always on the same subject, and I always holding him to John 6:37.

One day, I met him in the hall of the institute and made up my mind that the time had come to battle it out. I told him to sit down, and I sat down beside him. "Do you believe the Bible?" I asked.

"Yes," he replied, "I believe everything in it."

"Do you believe John 6:37?"

"Yes, I believe everything in the Bible."

"Do you believe that Jesus Christ told the truth when He said, '*Him that cometh to me I will in no wise cast out*'?"

"Yes, I do; I believe everything in the Bible," he answered.

"Well then, will you come?"

"I have committed the unpardonable sin."

I replied, "Jesus does not say, 'Him that hath not committed the unpardonable sin that cometh to Me I will in no wise cast out.' He says, '*Him that cometh to me I will in no wise cast out.*'"

"But I have sinned willfully after I have received the knowledge of the truth."

"Jesus does not say, 'Him that hath not sinned willfully after he received the knowledge of the truth that cometh unto Me I will in no wise cast out.' He says, '*Him that cometh to me I will in no wise cast out.*'"

"But I have been once enlightened and have tasted the heavenly gift but have fallen away, and it is impossible to renew me again unto repentance."

"Jesus does not say, 'If Him that hath not tasted of the heavenly gift and hath not fallen away cometh to Me, I will in no wise cast him out.' He says, '*Him that cometh to me I will in no wise cast out.*'"

"But I am possessed of the devil," he rebutted.

"Jesus does not say, 'Him that is not possessed of the devil that cometh to Me I will in no wise cast out.' He says, '*Him that cometh to me I will in no wise cast out.*'"

"I mean that the devil has entered into me as he had into Judas Iscariot."

"Jesus does not say, 'Him that the devil hath not entered into, as he did into Judas Iscariot, that cometh to Me I will in no wise cast out.' He says, *'Him that cometh to me I will in no wise cast out.'*"

"But my heart is hard as a millstone."

"Jesus does not say, 'Him that hath a soft and tender heart that cometh to Me I will in no wise cast out.' He says, *'Him that cometh to me I will in no wise cast out.'*"

"But I do not know that I have any desire to come."

"Jesus does not say, 'Him that hath a desire to come, and comes unto Me, I will in no wise cast out.' He says, *'Him that cometh to me I will in no wise cast out.'*"

"But I do not know that I can come in the right way."

"Jesus does not say, 'Him that cometh to Me in the right way I will in no wise cast out.' He says, *'Him that cometh to me I will in no wise cast out.'*"

"Well, I don't know that I care to come."

"Jesus does not say, 'Him that careth to come to Me, and comes to Me, I will in no wise cast out.' He says, *'Him that cometh to me I will in no wise cast out.'*"

The man's excuses and subterfuges were exhausted. I looked him square in the face and said, "Now, will you come? Get down on your knees and quit your nonsense." He knelt, and I knelt by his side. "Now," I said, "follow me in prayer. 'Lord Jesus,'" I said.

He repeated, "Lord Jesus."

"My heart is as hard as a millstone."

"My heart is as hard as a millstone."

"I have no desire to come unto Thee."

"I have no desire to come unto Thee."

"But Thou hast said in Thy Word...."

"But Thou hast said in Thy Word...."

"'*Him that cometh to me I will in no wise cast out.*'"

"'*Him that cometh to me I will in no wise cast out.*'"

"Now, the best I know how, I come."

"Now, the best I know how, I come."

"Thou hast said, '*Him that cometh to me I will in no wise cast out.*'"

"Thou hast said, '*Him that cometh to me I will in no wise cast out.*'"

"I believe this statement of Thine."

"I believe this statement of Thine."

"Therefore, though I don't feel it, I believe Thou hast received me."

"Therefore, though I don't feel it, I believe Thou hast received me."

When he had finished, I said, "Did you really come?"

He replied, "I did."

"Has He received you?"

"I do not feel it," he replied.

"But what does He say?"

He answered, "'*Him that cometh to me I will in no wise cast out.*'"

"Is this true? Does Jesus tell the truth, or does He lie?"

"He tells the truth."

"What, then, must He have done?"

"He must have received me."

"Now," I said, "go to your room. Stand firmly upon this promise of Jesus Christ. The devil will give you an awful conflict, but just answer him every time with John 6:37 and stand right there, believing what Jesus says in spite of your feelings, in spite of what the devil may say, in spite of everything."

He went to his room. The devil did give him an awful conflict, but he stood firmly on John 6:37, and later he came out of his room triumphant and radiant.

Years have passed since then. Though the devil has tried again and again to plunge him into despair, he has stood firmly on John 6:37, and today he is being used of God to do larger work for Christ than that of any man I know. He is the author of the hymn that goes,

> Years I spent in vanity and pride,
> Caring not my Lord was crucified,
> Knowing not it was for me He died
> On Calvary.
>
> Mercy there was great, and grace was free;
> Pardon there was multiplied to me;
> There my burdened soul found liberty—
> At Calvary.[3]

Last, anyone can be saved who will come to Jesus. *"The Spirit and the bride say, Come. And let him that heareth say, Come. And let him that is athirst come. And whosoever will, let him take the water of life freely"* (Revelation 22:17).

Come now, come.

---

3. William Reed Newell, "At Calvary," 1895.

HOW TO FIND REST

"Come unto me, all ye that labor and are heavy laden,
and I will give you rest. Take my yoke upon you,
and learn of me; for I am meek and lowly in heart:
and ye shall find rest unto your souls."
—Matthew 11:28–29

My subject in this chapter is just the offer this world needs. You will find it in Matthew 11:28: *"Come unto me, all ye that labor and are heavy laden, and I will give you rest."* That is just the offer this old world needs. What this world needs is rest. If he or she has not already found it in Christ, what every man and woman needs is rest. When I see the millions of men and women on the earth who toil hard for small pay, and who go home night after night to their wretched dwellings, all worn out, without any fit place to sleep—when I see them, my heart is heavy; but when I see the many more millions, rich as well as poor, who have not only no rest for the body but no rest for the heart, no rest for the soul, my heart is heavier yet. But I am glad that there is One who can give rest to every tired heart, and that One is Jesus Christ. He stands today with extended hands and says, *"Come unto me, all ye that labor and are heavy laden, and I will give you rest."* Now, those are either the words of a divine Being or the words of a lunatic.

If the Lord Jesus Christ offers and gives rest, He is a divine Being; if He offers rest and cannot give it, He is a lunatic. Suppose any man, even the greatest and the best that the world had ever seen, should stand and hold out his hands to this sorrowing, grief-stricken, burdened world of ours and say what Jesus said: "Come unto Me, and I will give you rest." You would know at once that the man had gone crazy, for no man can do it. But Jesus offers to do it, and He does it. Thousands, tens of thousands, millions throughout the centuries have accepted Christ's offer, and everyone who has accepted it has found rest.

There was a great throng of people present when the Lord Jesus spoke that day, a motley crowd, representing much misery. There were multitudes of poor and sick people there, representing all kinds of diseases—leprosy, blindness, and so forth. The demoniac was there, as well as the outcast, the downcast, and those who were trampled upon—a vast mass of misery—and the Lord Jesus Christ cast His loving eye over that great multitude that represented so much misery, and His great heart went out to them, and He said, "Come, come to Me, every one of you who has a burden, everyone who has a sorrow, everyone who has a broken heart; come unto Me, all who labor and are heavy laden, and I will give you rest."

And do you know, men and women, He not only extended His hands to that great throng that represented so much misery, but He also extends His hands to men and women of all ages who are burdened, downtrodden, oppressed, wretched, brokenhearted, and despairing. He says to them all, *"Come unto me, all ye that labor and are heavy laden, and I will give you rest."* He says it to you today.

Will you please notice, in the first place, who it is He has invited—all who labor and are heavy laden. Commentators have tried to tone down the words of our Lord. Some tell us that He meant all who were burdened with the many requirements of the Mosaic law; others tell us that He meant all who were burdened by a consciousness of sin, or a sense of guilt. But, friends, He means just what He said: *"Come unto me, **all** ye that labor"*—every man who has a burden, a sorrow, a heartache, a trouble, a woe of any kind—Jesus invites you to come.

Come, All Who Are Burdened with Sin and Shame

First of all, He invites all who are burdened with a sense of sin and a sense of shame. I suppose there are many of you who have been brought, in one way or another, to recognize the fact that your life is disgraceful. You are ashamed of yourself. You hardly lift up your head; you dare not lift it up and look your fellow men or fellow women in the face. You say to yourself, *My life is simply shameful,* and you are crushed by the sense of your disgrace and sin. To every one of you, Jesus says, *"Come unto me,…and I will give you rest."*

That day when our Lord Jesus uttered these words in Capernaum, on the outskirts of the crowd was a woman who was a sinner, a professional sinner, an outcast despised by everyone. I have no doubt that many a woman who prided herself on her morality turned round and looked at her with scorn as she stood there. Soon, Jesus looked at her, too—not with scorn but with pity, with compassion, with tenderness, with yearning, with love. It seems that when His eye fell upon her, she looked right at Him and saw that He was speaking directly to her. He seemed to lose sight of everybody else and just stretch His hands out toward her as He uttered the words of the text: "*Come unto me, all ye that labor and are heavy laden, and I will give you rest.*"

That woman said, "He means me," and when the crowd broke up, she followed Jesus at a distance to see where He was going. Jesus arrived at the house of Simon the Pharisee, who had invited Him to dinner. As soon as she knew where He had gone, she hurried to her home, took out of her treasures a very costly box of ointment—the most expensive thing that she had—returned to Simon's house, and went into the open door through the open court; and, as Jesus reclined, there in the Oriental way, she came up behind Him, bent over His feet, which were bare in the Oriental fashion, and began to bathe them with her tears.

The other guests looked up at her in scorn. They said, "This man pretends to be a prophet; He is no prophet, or He would not allow that woman to touch Him. If He were a prophet, He would know what kind of a woman she is, that she is a sinner." Well, He did know. He knew better than any of them did, not only that she was a sinner, but that she was a repentant sinner. When His feet were wet with her tears, she took the long tresses of her beautiful hair and wiped His feet with her hair. Then she broke the alabaster box of precious ointment over them, and the Lord Jesus turned to her and said, "*Thy sins are forgiven*" (Luke 7:48). Then He said again, "*Woman, thy faith hath saved thee; go in peace*" (verse 50); and that woman, who that day had stood on the outskirts of the crowd with a broken heart, went away from that house with the rest of God in her heart. Is there any woman reading this like her, or any man down in sin—anyone burdened with a sense of sin and shame? Come to the Lord Jesus Christ, and He will give you rest.

Come, All Who Are Burdened with the Bondage of Sin

In the second place, the Lord Jesus invites every man and woman who is burdened with the bondage of sin. There are men, for example, who are in bondage to the appetite of strong drink. You want to be sober, you want to lead upright lives, you have tried again and again to give up the drink, but you have failed. And this appetite for strong drink is an awful, crushing burden. Some of you are burdened with the appetite for morphine or cocaine or heroin or other drugs. Oh, how you have tried to be freed from your bondage. The Lord Jesus says, *"Come unto me,…and I will give you rest."* Some of you are burdened with vileness, with impurity, with disgusting sin. How you hate yourself, how you despise yourself, how you have tried to break away, time and time again, until at last you have given it up and are utterly discouraged, crushed by the power of your sin. Jesus says, *"Come unto me,…and I will give you rest."* For the rest of you, it is some other sin; but if we could read the secret sorrow of your heart, we would find hundreds of men and women crushed to the earth by the power of sin. The Lord Jesus says to every one of you, *"Come unto me, all ye that labor and are heavy laden, and I will give you rest."*

I have a very dear friend in America who was very carefully reared by a godly mother who was very much afraid that he would become a drunkard, and so she besought him that he would never touch alcoholic liquor. He lived in the country, and one day, he went to town with a man. On the way back, the man bought some whiskey and asked him to drink. "No," he replied, "I promised my mother never to drink."

"Well," the man said, "if you don't drink, you will insult me." And that elderly man just worked on that boy until he got him to drink his first glass of whiskey, at the age of eighteen. Then the demon in him was set on fire. From that day on, he became almost immediately a drunkard. He went down, down, down, in the course of years, losing one position after another, and at last was a wrecked man in New York City. He had uttered 138 forgeries against his last employer, and the officers of the law were now in search of him.

One night, one awful night, he went into a bar and, for a long time, sat there in a drunken stupor on a whiskey keg. Coming out of the stupor, he felt all the horrors of delirium tremens coming over him. He thought he was going to die. He went up to the bar and ordered a glass of whiskey, then rattled his glass upon the bar so that the bar shook. He said, "Men, hear me, hear me; I shall never drink another glass of whiskey if I die." And they all laughed at him.

He went out of the bar to the lockup and said to the sergeant of police at the desk, "Lock me up; I am going to have the tremens; lock me up!" The sergeant sent him down to the cell and locked him up. He spent a night of awful agony, and the next day, as the night was coming on, somebody said to him, "Why don't you go to Jerry McAuley's Mission?" The lockup was a little ways from the mission. So, as best he could, in an awful condition, he went down to Jerry McAuley's Cremorne Mission and listened to the testimony of one man's salvation after another; and when Jerry McAuley asked all who would take Christ to come to the front, he went up to the front, knelt down, and said, "Jerry, pray for me."

Jerry said, "Pray for yourself."

"Oh," he said, "I don't know how to pray. I have forgotten how to pray. Jerry, pray for me."

Jerry repeated, "Pray for yourself," and that wrecked and ruined man lifted up his broken heart to Jesus. He came to Jesus; Jesus met him then and there and took away his appetite for whiskey.

Today, that man is one of the most honored men in New York City. Some years ago, I was in the city of Washington, and I met the postmaster general of the United States. He asked me if I would go to dinner with him that night after a meeting. I agreed, and as I entered his drawing room, whom should I see sitting there as an honored guest but Mr. Samuel Hadley, the poor drunkard of bygone years of whom I have just spoken, who was now an honored guest in the house of the postmaster general of the United States of America.

Oh, men, are you burdened? Have you fought against sin and failed? Have you tried again and again, perhaps signed pledge after pledge, only to break it? Have you some other besetting sin? Are you burdened with the weight of an overcoming sin? Jesus holds out His hand to you today. He says, *"Come unto me, all ye that labor and are heavy laden, and I will give you rest."*

He invites everybody burdened with a sorrow. Perhaps some of you have recently lost a spouse, and all the light has gone out of you. Some of you sons and daughters are brokenhearted over the recent death of your loving Christian mother. Some of you fathers and mothers are brokenhearted because a beloved child has recently been taken from your home and sleeps tonight in the quiet cemetery. Some of you have met with reverses in business. Some of you have other sorrows. But it matters not what your sorrow is, how peculiar, how great, how overwhelming. To every sorrowing man and woman, Jesus holds out His hands and says, *"Come unto me,…and I will give you rest."*

Some time ago, in our country, there was a gentleman and his wife who had a very happy home. The man was prosperous in business in Cleveland, Ohio; but there came a reverse in business, and the man lost everything he had in the world. His home was broken up, and his oldest daughter had to go out to work to make a living. His two boys were too young to work. His wife had to leave him and take the two boys to the home of a sister in one of the Southern states, where she worked as a housekeeper to make a living for herself and the boys.

The father came to Chicago to see if he could retrieve his fortunes. After his wife had been in the South for some time, hoping that a better day might come again, she received a telegraphic dispatch saying that her husband was very ill, and she had better come at once. She took the train and reached Chicago that night, then went to the hospital to which her husband had been taken. But, by some mistake, the authorities of the hospital said to her, "You cannot see your husband tonight; come at nine o'clock tomorrow morning, and you can see him."

With a heavy heart, she returned to a place where she stopped, then went back to the hospital at nine the next morning. When she rang the bell, the authorities met her at the door and said, "Your husband died last night." She took him out and buried him, but so great were her loneliness and sorrow, and so frequent her weeping, that they affected her eyesight. She went to a physician, who said that her condition was not very serious and that she could go back to Mississippi, for her eyes would soon be well.

She supposed that he was a regular physician but found out afterward that he was a Christian Science physician and was trying to cure her by making her feel that she was not ill. She went back to Mississippi, and her eyes got worse and worse. She went to a regular physician, who examined her eyes and said, "Madam, your case is hopeless. If you had come to me a few weeks ago, I could have helped you. Your trouble has gone so far now that there is absolutely no hope for you. You will be totally blind."

Home broken up, husband buried, eyesight gone, she returned to Chicago. She dropped into our church, where she heard the gospel. She came to Jesus with all her overwhelming sorrow, and

He gave her rest. And if you come to the prayer meeting at our church any Friday night, you will see sitting there a woman with a refined, beautiful face, dressed in black, eyes closed, perfectly sightless; but in that face, you will see a serener and profounder joy than perhaps you have ever seen in a human face. Very likely you will see her rise to her feet in the course of the meeting with a face radiant with the sunshine of heaven, and she will tell of how wonderfully God has blessed her; and you may hear her say what she says often, that she thanks God she has lost her sight, for out of her great troubles, she was brought to Christ and found a joy that she never knew before.

Men and women, there is a place where there is a cure for every sorrow. That place is at the feet of Jesus. I have a beautiful Testament at home that I think very highly of, not because of the beauty of the binding, but because my mother gave it to my grandmother, my father's mother—I think it was at the time of my grandfather's death—and on the flyleaf of the Testament, in my mother's own beautiful handwriting, are these words: "Earth hath no sorrow that heaven cannot heal." That is true, but something better is true: Earth has no sorrow that Jesus cannot heal right now, even before we get to heaven.

Come, All Who Are Burdened with Doubt and Unbelief

Again, the Lord Jesus invites all who are burdened with doubt and unbelief. Now, to some men, doubt and unbelief are not a burden. They are glad that they are skeptics. They are proud of their doubts. But to an earnest-minded man, to a man of any real moral earnestness, doubt is a burden, a heavy load—he is never proud of doubt. He never rejoices in doubt. An earnest-minded man does not want to doubt but to trust; not uncertainty but certainty; not agnosticism but knowledge of God. I believe that there are some of you who honestly doubt, and your doubt is a burden.

Well, Jesus says to you, "Come unto Me, all ye that are burdened with doubt, and I will give you rest."

"What," you say, "a skeptic come to Christ, an unbeliever come to Christ, an agnostic come to Christ?" Certainly! He is the best One you can come to. Thomas was a skeptic. He was not with the other disciples when they saw our Lord after His resurrection. "*The other disciples therefore said unto* [Thomas], *We have seen the Lord. But he said unto them, Except I shall see in his hands the print of the nails, and put my finger into the print of the nails, and thrust my hand into his side, I will not believe*" (John 20:25). But Thomas was an honest doubter, and when he thought that perhaps the Lord Jesus would be around the next Sunday evening, he was there. He came to Jesus with his doubts. Jesus scattered every one of them, and Thomas cried, "*My Lord and my God*" (John 20:28).

Nathaniel was a doubter, an honest doubter, a thoroughgoing skeptic. Philip came to him and said, "*We have found him, of whom Moses in the law, and the prophets, did write, Jesus of Nazareth, the son of Joseph*" (John 1:45). Nathaniel said, "I don't believe He is the Messiah. He came from Nazareth; He is not the Messiah. '*Can there any good thing come out of Nazareth?*'" (John 1:46). Philip said, "*Come and see*" (verse 46). Ah, that is the thing to do—come and see. Nathaniel accompanied Philip and met the Lord, and he had not been with the Lord ten minutes when all his doubts were gone, and he cried, "*Thou art the Son of God; thou art the King of Israel*" (John 1:49).

Men, if you are burdened with doubt, bring it to Jesus. Whatever your burden is, Jesus invites you—every burdened, heavyhearted one—to come unto Him. "*Come unto me,…and I will give you rest.*"

"Come unto Me"

Will you please notice what Jesus invites you to do? Jesus says, "*Come unto me*"—not "Come unto the church," for the church cannot give you rest. I believe in the church; I believe every converted man ought to be a member of some church; but the church never gave anybody rest. Today, the church is full of people who have never found rest. They have come to the church instead of coming to Jesus Himself.

Furthermore, Jesus does not say, "Come to a creed." I believe in creeds. I think every man ought to have a creed. A creed is simply an intelligent, systematic statement of what a man believes; and a man ought to believe something, and he ought to be able to state intelligently what he believes. And if he is an intelligent, studious man, his creed will be getting longer all the time. I have a creed, a great long one. It is getting longer every day, for I am learning something new every day; but, friends, no creed ever gave anybody rest. The Thirty-nine Articles won't give you rest. The Westminster Catechism, a good creed, won't give you rest. There was never a written or printed creed that gave anybody rest. It is not about going to a creed; it is about going to the personal Savior.

Many men are orthodox enough for anybody—having great long creeds—but they never come to the personal Jesus, and they do not find rest. The Lord Jesus does not say, "Come unto the pope," or "Come unto the priest," or "Come unto the preacher," or "Come unto the evangelist," or "Come unto any other man." He says, "*Come unto me*." No preacher can give you rest; no priest can give you rest; no pope can give you rest; no man can give you rest. Jesus says, "*Come unto me*."

I have sometimes asked people if they have come to Jesus, and they say, "Oh, I am a Protestant." Well, that never saved anybody. There will be lots of Protestants in hell. Others say, "I am a Roman Catholic." That never saved anybody, either. There will be lots of Roman Catholics in hell. When a man says, "I am a Roman Catholic," I say, "I am not asking you that. Have you come to Jesus?" It is not a question of whether you are a Roman Catholic or a Protestant. Have you come to Jesus? If you have not, will you come today?

Oh, men are so anxious to put somebody else in the place of Jesus—to come to some man. A lady said to me one night in my own church, "I am a Roman Catholic. I like to come to hear you preach, and I would like to ask you a question. Can I come and confess to you? I want to confess to somebody."

"No, you can't," I said. "Go to Jesus." "*Come unto me*," says Jesus. Nobody but Jesus can give you rest. Jesus can, and He will, give rest to anyone who comes to Him.

> *Come unto me, all ye that labor and are heavy laden, and I will give you rest. Take my yoke upon you, and learn of me; for I am meek and lowly in heart: and ye shall find rest unto your souls. For my yoke is easy, and my burden is light.*
>
> (Matthew 11:28–30)

Come to Jesus, take His yoke, surrender absolutely unto Him; commit all your sins to Him to pardon; commit all your doubts to Him to remove; commit all your thoughts to Him to teach; commit yourself to Him to believe in Him, to learn from Him, to obey Him, and to serve Him. The moment you come to Him with all your heart and cast yourself upon Him, He will give you rest. You can have rest right now, before this chapter comes to a close, right this moment. Jesus is nearer to you than a man sitting beside you. Say, "Jesus, I come," and He will give you rest.

One night in my church in Chicago, one of the church officers, going around the upper gallery after I had finished preaching and as the audience was going out, stepped up to a gentleman and asked him, "Are you saved?"

"Yes, sir," he said, "I am saved." He was very positive about it.

"How long have you been saved?"

He answered, "About five minutes."

He asked, "When were you saved?"

"About five minutes ago, while that man was preaching." He did not wait till I got through my sermon. He came to Jesus right there and then, and Jesus saved him right there.

Will you come? Lose sight of me, and see the Lord Jesus standing there, holding out His hands to you, one and all, with a heart bursting with love, breaking with pity and compassion, and saying to every heavyhearted man and woman, *"Come unto me, all ye that labor and are heavy laden, and I will give you rest."* Will you come?

"JOY UNSPEAKABLE AND FULL OF GLORY"

"Though now ye see him not, yet believing, ye rejoice with joy unspeakable and full of glory."
—1 Peter 1:8

Christians are the happiest people in the world. According to our text, they *"rejoice with joy unspeakable and full of glory,"* and nobody else does. I am going to tell you now why Christians are happy.

Forgiven of Sin

First of all, Christians are happy because they know that their sins are all forgiven. Nobody in this world knows that his sins are forgiven except a Christian. If any man or woman who is not a Christian says, "I know my sins are forgiven," he or she says what is untrue, for his or her sins are not forgiven. But every true Christian knows that his sins are forgiven—all of them. You ask, "How does he know that?" Because God says so. If you will turn to Acts 13:39, you will see that *"all that believe are justified from all things."* God says so.

A sinner came to Christ one day and washed His feet with her tears and wiped them with her hair. Men looked on in scorn, but Jesus turned to her and said, *"Thy sins are forgiven"* (Luke 7:48), and she left that place knowing that all her sins were forgiven. (See Luke 7:37–50.) She knew it because Jesus said so. And God says to every Christian, "Your are forgiven," just as distinctly as He said it to the woman.

Christians know their sins are forgiven in a second way— because the Holy Spirit bears witness in their hearts that their sins are forgiven. One day, the apostle Peter was preaching in the household of Cornelius and, speaking about Jesus, said, *"To him give all the prophets witness, that through his name whosoever believeth in him shall receive remission of sins"* (Acts 10:43). Cornelius and his whole household believed it, and immediately the Spirit of God came upon them.

When you and I believe in Jesus, His Spirit comes into our hearts and bears witness with our spirit that our sins are all forgiven, and that we are children of God. There is no joy on earth like the joy of knowing that God has forgiven and blotted out every sin we have ever committed.

Suppose a person was in prison for life after committing some crime, and someone brought him a pardon. Don't you think he would be happy? The governor of the state of Pennsylvania once decided to pardon a man, and he sent Mr. Moody to tell him that he was pardoned. Mr. Moody went to the prison. He was going to preach a sermon, but before he began, he said, "The governor of the state has handed me a pardon for one of you men." He was not going to tell them who it was till he got through the sermon. But as he looked over the crowd of men, he saw that there was such suspense and such agony, everyone wondering whether it was he, that he said, "This will never do in the world, to keep these men in suspense. I must tell them at once who the man is." So he said, "The man who is pardoned is —." And, oh! What joy filled that man's heart when he found that out of the great company of criminals, he was the one whom the governor had pardoned!

But, men, to know that one is pardoned here on earth is nothing compared to knowing that God has forgiven all your sins and blotted them all out. Oh, the joy that comes into the heart when a man knows that every sin he ever committed is pardoned and blotted out, and that God has absolutely nothing against him. A great king once wrote a song that has lived through the centuries. It is a song of joy. That great king had been a great sinner, and God had forgiven his sin. He had much to make a man happy. He was the greatest king of his day. He had great wealth, he had great armies, he was the greatest general of the time, and he had a great palace; but when he came to write his song of joy, he did not say, "Happy is the man who has a beautiful palace"; he did not say, "Happy is the man who has great armies"; he did not say, "Happy is the man who is a great general"; he did not say, "Happy is the man who is beloved by his people." He said, *"Blessed is he whose transgression is forgiven, whose sin is covered. Blessed is the man unto whom the LORD imputeth not iniquity, and in whose spirit there is no guile"* (Psalm 32:1–2). Every man here today who will take the Lord Jesus as his Savior will be forgiven all his sins and will have the joy of knowing that every sin is blotted out.

Set Free from Sin's Power

In the second place, Christians are happy because they are set free from sin's power. Now, everybody who sins is a slave to sin.

Years ago, when I was a boy in the Southern states, there were black slaves. Some of their masters were kind to them, and some of their masters were cruel—oh, so very, very cruel; it makes one's heart ache to think what those poor black men suffered! But there has never been a slave owner in the South who has been such a cruel master as Satan, and there has never been a bondage so awful as the bondage of sin.

Some people are bound by the appetite for strong drink; I presume some of you have tried to break away from drink time and time again, but you are enslaved by it. Some of you are enslaved by morphine, some by laudanum, some by cocaine, some by a bad temper, some by an ungovernable tongue, some by other things; but every man or woman without Christ is a slave. But when you come to Jesus Christ, He sets you free. He says, *"If ye continue in my word, then are ye my disciples indeed; and ye shall know the truth, and the truth shall make you free....If the Son therefore shall make you free, ye shall be free indeed"* (John 8:31–32, 36). The Lord Jesus Christ will set free every man and every woman who believes in Him from the power of sin, from the power of strong drink, from the power of a drug, from the power of bad temper, from the power of impurity, from the power of profanity, from the power of every sin.

I was reading the life story of a very dear friend of mine. I have read it a number of times before, but I read it again. In it, he told how, one night, after he had been a slave for years, he knelt down and prayed in a mission, and Jesus Christ met him and set him free. And he said, "From that till this I have never had the least desire for strong drink." When he left the mission that night, he knew that, after years of slavery and ruin, he was a free man. He just shouted for joy, "Glory to God!" and he has been shouting that ever since. I wish he were here today so that you might hear him shout and could look into his face. Oh, the joy of being set free from sin after days or weeks or months or even years of slavery.

Given an Identity

In the third place, Christians are happy because they know that they are children of God. It is a wonderful thing to know that you are a child of God. No one knows it but the Christian, for no one is a child of God but the Christian. You ask, "How does the Christian know that he is a child of God?" Because God says so. In John 1:12, He says that *"as many as received him, to them gave he power to become the sons of God, even to them that believe on his name."* Today, if you, man or woman, young or old, will take the Lord Jesus Christ, then the moment you do it, you will be a child of God—and you will know that you are a child of God. Isn't that enough to make you happy? Suppose you knew that you were the son of some great man—for example, the son of a millionaire, a king, or an emperor—don't you think you would be happy? But being the son of any millionaire, king, or emperor is nothing compared to being the son of God, the King of Kings.

One day, years ago, an English duke lay dying. He called his younger brother to his bedside and said, "Brother, in a few hours, you will be a duke, and I will be a king." He was a Christian, he was a child of a King, and he knew that when he left his dukedom down here, he would get a kingdom up there. And, friends, no matter how poor a person is—young or old—if he will take Jesus Christ, the moment he does, he can lift up his head and say, "I am a child of a King; I know I am a child of God."

Sometimes, as I travel around the world, people will point out a man to me and say, "That man is the son of such and such a great man." In Germany, a person points out another and says, "That is the son of such and such a king"; in another place, a person says, "That is the son of such and such a king." What of it? Suppose he is a child of a king; I am a child of God. That is better than to be a child of a king. Now, they suggest at church that you put money in the offering. Well, I guess that some of you cannot put money in, but I want to say that if you can't put money in, you are just as welcome as anybody; and if you can't put checks in, you are just as welcome as anybody. We read in the Bible that unto the poor, the gospel was preached. (See Luke 7:22.) I believe in preaching to the rich. They need it as much as anybody; but, thank God, the woman who sits in church today and has to walk there because she hasn't money enough to pay a penny to take the bus, the poorest woman there is, or the richest, can become a child of God in a moment, by taking Jesus Christ. I would rather be the poorest woman in the building who is a child of God than the richest woman in the building who is a child of the devil.

Delivered from All Fear

Again, Christians are happy because they are delivered from all fear. A true Christian who believes the Bible, and studies it and remembers it, is not afraid of anything or anybody. Now, a great many people who are very rich have all their joy spoiled because they are constantly thinking that some calamity may overtake them. Rich men don't enjoy their riches because they are afraid of losing them, and people who have friends around them don't enjoy their friends because they are afraid they will die. People who have all the comforts of life don't enjoy them because they fear that some calamity may come and sweep them away. On the other hand, those with very little, who are perhaps just getting by, don't enjoy it because they fear they may be thrown out of work and not be able to make a living. But true Christians are delivered from all fear. There is one verse in the Bible that, if you are a child of God and you believe it and keep it in mind, will take away all anxiety as long as you live. That is Romans 8:28, which says, *"We know that all things work together for good to them that love God."*

Sometimes, the devil whispers to me, "Perhaps you will lose everything you have in the world." "Well," I say, "it doesn't make any difference if I do. If I do, that will be one of the *'all things,'* and *'all things work together for good.'"*

Sometimes, when I am away from my family, the devil whispers to me, "Your wife is ill," or "Your son is ill," or "Your daughters are ill and will die before you ever see them." I don't know how often the devil has come and whispered that. When he does, I just lift up my head and say, "Well, that cannot be, unless it is the will of God, my Father. And if they do die, it is one of the *'all things'* that work together for good."

Sometimes the devil comes and whispers, "Perhaps you will be taken ill; perhaps you may lose your eyesight or your hearing, and not be able to preach anymore." I just lift up my head and say, "Well, if I do, it will be one of the *'all things,'* and *'all things work together for good to them that love God.'"*

So, you see, if a person is a real Christian who believes the Bible and bears it in mind, he is not afraid of calamity; neither is he afraid of any man. Oh, so many people are afraid of men, tormented by the fear of men. A great many of you today would come out as Christians, but you are afraid that if you do, some man or woman might see you, and you are afraid that you will be laughed at, that you will be persecuted at the office or in the factory or at the shop. But a Christian is not afraid of man. The Christian reads Romans 8:31 and says, *"If God be for us, who can be against us?"* A Christian does not fear the face of any man or woman on earth.

In Chicago, a man came to me and said, "You had better look out—there is a man who says he has it in for you." He told me who the man was—a very desperate man, a man willing to do almost anything. Well, I was not troubled a bit. I did not lie awake a single night; I was not troubled two seconds. I said, "That is all right. I know he is quite powerful, and I have reason to believe he is unprincipled; but I know that I am right with God, that God is on my side. If God has undertaken to take care of me, that man can't touch me, unless it is God's will." I tell you, friends, a living faith in Jesus Christ will forever take away all fear of man.

It will take away the fear of death. I know so many people whose lives are just shadowed and darkened by the fear of death. Right in the midst of health and strength, they say, "Oh, if I should be taken with consumption, if I should get heart disease, if I should have diphtheria or smallpox or some other terrible disease...." But a Christian is not afraid of death. The Christian has lost all terrors of death. A Christian knows that what men call death is simply an opportunity for him to depart and be with Christ.

One evening in Chicago, I went over to see a young lady who had sung in my choir—a very beautiful, attractive girl whose life had been full of promise, but who had been suddenly cut down by rapid consumption. As it turned out, she did not have a day to live. I had been told that she would like to see me, so I went over to see her. I went into the room where the young girl, cut down in the very blossom of young womanhood, was lying upon her dying bed. I sat down by her, and her face shone like an angel's. I said to her, "Humanly speaking, there is no hope for your recovery."

She replied, "I know; I don't care to recover. I would have been glad to have recovered to serve Christ, if it had been His will; but since He has decided I can't recover and must very soon leave this world, I wanted to see you and tell you that I don't fear death. I am looking forward to what men call death with great joy and with great anticipation."

I went to my church to preach, and when I got up into the pulpit, someone brought me a note. That dying girl had asked for paper, and she had written a note and sent it over to the choir of the church, telling them how happy she was as she lay face-to-face with death and eternity. Oh, I tell you, friends, it is a joyful thing to have no fear of death.

Then, a Christian is delivered from fear of eternity. Now, to people without Christ, eternity is a dreadful thing to think about; but for people in Christ, eternity is about the sweetest thing there is to think about. There is a word that fills the heart of the Christian with joy and the heart of the unsaved with terror. That word is *eternity*. Oh, I love the word *eternity*, where all sorrow is over forever, as well as all separation, all sickness, and all death—where all is eternal sunshine. How I love the word *eternity*. But some of you don't love it. I have received letters from people who say they wish that I would not talk so much about eternity. I heard of one man who did not want to come to the meetings because I talked so much of eternity. But Christians like for me to talk of eternity. If you write out a card with the question "Where will you spend eternity?" and hand it to a man who is not a Christian, it will make him mad; hand it to a Christian, and it will make him glad. He will answer, "Why, I will spend eternity with Christ in glory."

Given Life Forevermore

That leads me to the next reason why Christians are happy. It is because they know that they will live forever. Oh, it is a wonderful thing to know that you will never die; that, throughout the endless ages of God, you will live on and on and on. As we read in 1 John 2:17, *"The world passeth away, and the lust thereof: but he that doeth the will of God abideth for ever."* And we read in John 3:36, *"He that believeth on the Son hath everlasting life: and he that believeth not the Son shall not see life; but the wrath of God abideth on him."*

Before I was a Christian, I did not like to look into the future; but how I love to look into the future now! Very often, I sit in my room and say, "I wonder how many years I will have to preach."

Well, I can't have very many at the outside—probably about twenty, possibly twenty-five, barely possibly thirty years. That is not very much, and then what? Eternity! That is better than preaching. It is a great joy to preach; but, oh, to be able to stand and look down at the coming ages and see them roll on, age upon age, age upon age, and age upon age, knowing that you are going to live for all eternity in happiness and joy ever increasing! I don't wonder that Christians are happy. I don't wonder that they have "*joy unspeakable and* [are] *full of glory*" (1 Peter 1:8).

Heirs of God and Joint-Heirs with Christ

There are two other reasons why Christians are happy. The next one is because they know that they are heirs—heirs of God and joint-heirs with Jesus Christ. They know that they have an incorruptible and undefiled inheritance that fades not away, laid up in store in heaven for them. Suppose a person rides down a beautiful English country road and sees beautiful mansions and manor houses, as well as lakes, forests, parks, and gardens, and says, "It must be very pleasant to live in there." Well, I suppose it is, but how long will the inhabitants live there? The father of the family will probably live ten years—twenty, perhaps; the children will live forty or fifty, possibly sixty. Soon gone, soon gone. But, friends, every man, woman, and child today who will take Jesus will have an inheritance that will last forever—an incorruptible and undefiled inheritance that fades not away. Every earthly inheritance soon fails—even the richest man on earth won't keep his property very long. But the poorest man or woman here today, young or old, who will take Jesus Christ will get an inheritance that will last forever.

One day, a poor English girl, very plainly dressed, was riding along in a third-class carriage and looking out the window. She passed by beautiful farms, beautiful trees, and beautiful mansions;

and every little while, a man who sat near her heard her say, "That belongs to my Father." They would come to a farm, and she would say, "That belongs to my Father"; then to a beautiful mansion house, and she would say, "That belongs to my Father, too"; then they would pass a lordly castle, and she would say, "That belongs to my Father." Finally, the man turned to her and said, "Well, miss, you must have a rich father, for you have been saying for miles as we passed along, 'That belongs to my father.' Your father must own a great deal of property. He must be a very rich man." She said, "He is—I am a child of God." She was very rich, indeed.

Men and women, listen. Some of you are having a pretty hard time down in this world. I suppose you have to work long hours for small pay. Your homes are not very comfortable. Well, I want to tell you, you won't have to live in them very long; and if you will take Christ, you are going to such a mansion as this earth never saw, to such an inheritance as no man ever inherited on this earth. When you go by the rich man's mansion, you say, "I wish I had a home like that." Even if you did, you could not keep it long. If you will take Jesus Christ, you will be an heir to all that God has. The whole world belongs to Him—the cattle on a thousand hills—and if you are a child of God, if you will take Christ, you will be an heir to all He is and all He has; you can become an heir today.

Blessed with the Holy Spirit

There is one more reason why Christians are happy. That is because God gives to Christians the Holy Spirit to dwell in their heart; and when the Holy Spirit dwells in their heart, He fills it with sunshine, gladness, and joy unspeakable.

One Monday morning, a poor woman came to my door, rang the bell, and said she wanted to see me. The girl who answered the door said, "You know he sees no one on Monday."

She said, "I know it, but I have got to see him."

So the girl called me down; and when I arrived, I saw one of the members of my church—a poor washerwoman who had to work hard for her living. "Oh," she said, "Mr. Torrey, I know you don't see anybody on Monday, and I didn't want to trouble you, but I received the Holy Spirit last night. I could not sleep all night, and I made up my mind that I was going to give up one day's work and just come round and tell you how happy I was. I just had to. I can't very well afford to give up a day's work, but my heart is so full of joy, I could not keep still. I had to tell somebody, and I didn't know anybody else I wanted to tell as much as I wanted to tell you. Though I knew you don't see anybody on Monday, I thought you would be glad to have me come and tell you."

"Yes," I affirmed, "I am glad."

That woman was so happy that she could not work; her heart was full of joy.

So, I don't care how dark your heart is today, how full of sadness it is, how full of bitterness, how hopeless. If you will really take Jesus Christ as your Savior and surrender your whole heart and your whole life to Him as your Lord and Master, your heart will be filled with sweetness above anything to be known this side of heaven.

Only real Christians rejoice with joy unspeakable and full of glory. Just going to church won't do it; just saying your prayers won't do it; just reading your catechism won't do it; just reading the Bible won't do it; just reading the prayer book won't do it; just being baptized won't do it; just being confirmed won't do it; just going to the Lord's Supper won't do it; but if you will take Jesus into your heart to be your Savior and to rule and reign there, and surrender all to Him, I guarantee that every one of you will get a joy that is like heaven here below.

People say to me, "Do you expect to go to heaven?" Yes, I know I am going to heaven; but, thank God, I am in heaven now. I have a present heaven until I go to the future heaven. I feel like singing all the time. I used to be one of the bluest men on earth. I was constitutionally blue. I was despondent and gloomy. I inherited it from both sides. Oh, I used to sit and have the blues by the hour. But, do you know, I have never had the blues since I really took the Lord Jesus. I have had trouble; I have had losses; I have seen everything I had in the world swept away, so I had nothing left; I have seen the time when I had a wife and four children and not a penny to buy them the next meal. But it came in time, for I knew where to go—right to God. I have seen times when I didn't know where the rent for the house was coming from, or the wood for the fire in a bitter, cold winter. But I was happy. I have been in a foreign country where I could not speak the language, and, some way or other, there was a failure of supplies, and I was absolutely penniless in a foreign city with a wife and child, hardly knowing anybody in the whole place. But I was happy. I knew Whom I trusted. I knew He would get me out somehow—and He did.

Oh, if you want darkness turned into sunshine, if you want sadness turned into joy, if you want despair turned into glory, if you want defeat turned into victory, if you want all that is bad turned into all that is good—take the Lord Jesus Christ, and take Him right now.

12

"THE FEAR OF MAN BRINGETH A SNARE"

"The fear of man bringeth a snare: but whoso putteth his trust in the LORD shall be safe."
—Proverbs 29:25

In life, we can go one of two ways—one of ruin, the other of salvation. *"The fear of man brings a snare"*—ruin! ruin! *"But whoso putteth his trust in the LORD shall be safe"*—the way of salvation, trust in Jehovah. Even if you do not believe another verse in the Bible, you know that this verse is true. Every man, I don't care how much of an infidel he may be, knows that the fear of man brings a snare. How many people there are who have been snared by the fear of man! How many young women there are who have come to the city from a country village innocent, guileless, pure, and upright, but loving gaiety; and, in coming to the city, they have sought gaiety where poor women are likely to seek it—in the theatre, at the dance clubs—but meaning no ill.

Loss of Dignity

One night, a woman returns from a dance with a young man in whom she has become interested, and who has been kind to her, and he makes an advance that the modest woman resents. She colors up. She is indignant. He laughs at her and says, "Oh, you don't understand. I don't mean anything wrong. Everyone does this in the city. You know, city life is gayer than country life. You don't understand—that is all." So she permits what she at first resented.

A few nights afterward, he goes a little further. Again, she is indignant, and again he laughs at her—laughs her out of her "puritanical scruples," as he calls them. Then he goes even further, and tonight, that girl is on the street, ruined, dishonored, belonging to the most wretched class that lives—the outcasts. The fear of man, the fear of someone's ridicule, has brought a snare that has landed that woman in the slums.

Alcoholism

A young man moves to Birmingham. He knows enough about life to know that any use of intoxicating liquor is dangerous in the day in which you and I live. His father and mother brought him up with the habits of temperance and total abstinence, and in coming to the city, he resolves that he will never visit a bar, that he will never drink even a glass of beer or wine. But one night, he is out with his new friends, enjoying some entertainment. After the entertainment is over, they propose going to a bar for just one glass of beer. "No," he says, "I never drink; it is perilous to drink.

I was brought up a total abstainer, and I intend to remain a total abstainer till the day of my death."

They laugh at him. "Oh," they say, "be a man. Nobody but a milksop is a total abstainer. If you want to amount to anything in Birmingham, you must take an occasional glass of beer. Of course, we don't want you to go to excess. We don't believe in intemperance, but one glass of beer won't hurt you. Come, be a man."

So the man has his first glass of beer, and it rouses the demon that is in him. That leads to another and another and another and many anothers; and, tonight, that young fellow is a bloated, ruined, penniless drunkard on the streets of Birmingham. The fear of man brought a snare that ruined his life.

A few weeks ago, I received from a friend one of the saddest letters I ever received. It was a letter from his brother's wife. My friend's brother was a very brilliant man, a man of the greatest promise, of extraordinary promise; but he got to drinking. He found that the drink was fastening itself upon him, and so he broke off and became a total abstainer. He had occasion to go to London to visit a very well-known man, whom many people knew by name. That man was in the way of promoting him to great honor. When he visited this man, he was offered a glass of wine at his table. He didn't dare offend his powerful friend by refusing the glass of wine, and he thought, *It is only one glass.* He took it and then went mad. He rushed from the house, went to one bar and then to another, and for days, his friends did not know where he was. They sent detectives on his track, who found him helplessly drunk in one of the lowest dens in London, and he has been drinking ever since. His brokenhearted wife wrote my friend, his brother: "He is crazy. He has gone and ruined his family; his home is broken up; all our prospects are blighted; he is lost; he is mad." The fear of man brought a snare.

Gambling

A young fellow comes to this city who is too much of a man to gamble—for no man who gambles is much of a man in that direction—but he likes an occasional innocent game of cards. One night, he is playing cards with his friends, and someone suggests that they put up just a threepenny bit to make it interesting. That is all. "Oh," the friend says, "we don't care for the money, but it is just to lend interest to the game."

"No," he says, "I never gamble. I think gambling is stealing." He is right, for gambling is stealing. No self-respecting man will gamble, for no self-respecting man wants another man's money. I don't see how a man who has taken another man's money by gambling can look in the mirror. I should think he would be ashamed to look himself in the face. He says, "No, gambling is rank dishonesty. I never gamble."

"Oh," a friend says, "it is not gambling; it is just for a little amusement. You better go home and go to Sunday school. Go and sit with your mother." And the group laughs him into his first game of cards for money. The gambler's passion—a harder passion to overcome than the appetite for drink ever was—seizes him, and tonight he is behind prison bars, because he gambled until he took his employer's money to gamble with. The fear of man brought a snare that has landed him in prison.

Denial of the Lord

Again, the fear of man ensnares Christians and causes them to deny their Lord. It did so to Peter. After Peter had just told his Lord that though all forsake Him, he never would, he said to a servant girl who accused him of being a follower of Jesus of Nazareth, "I don't know what you're talking about." (See Matthew 26:70.)

Then, a few moments after, he denied and, an hour after, with oaths and cursing, frightened by what someone might do or say, he denied his Lord a third time. (See Matthew 26:74.) Oh, but thank God, the time came when Peter threw his fear to the wind and stood before the very men who condemned Jesus to death, confessing his Lord and rebuking their sin.

Many of you are doing the same every day. Down in your office or shop or factory or mill, Jesus Christ is ridiculed. Harsh things are said about the Bible; the name of the Lord who died upon the cross of Calvary for you is taken in blasphemy; and you are not man enough, you are not woman enough, to stand up and to say, "I am a Christian. I believe in that Christ whom you are ridiculing. I believe in that Bible you are laughing at." You are afraid to be laughed at, and the fear of man has ensnared you into a denial of the Lord who died on the cross for you.

Compromise with the World

Again, the fear of man ensnares professed Christians into a guilty compromise with the world. How many professed Christians are doing things in family life, social life, and business life that you know are wrong? Your best moral judgment condemns you every time you do them, but you say, "Well, everybody does them. I will be considered odd if I don't do them, too. I will be ostracized from my set."

A Christian man in America, living in one of the suburbs of Chicago, where there is a great deal of the form of godliness but very little of the real power thereof, said to me, "My daughter is practically ostracized in this suburb because she won't dance, play cards, or go to the theatre." Thank God, she was woman enough, young girl though she was, to be disliked rather than to compromise. A lot of you are not. You would rather not go to the bar—you don't feel happy there. You would rather not play cards—you know the peril of it. You know how many family card parties have been the door through which sons have become gamblers. You would rather not dance. Your better self is shocked, as the modesty of every intelligent thinking woman must be shocked, at what you see in every dance club—a familiarity of contact permitted between the sexes that is permitted nowhere else in decent society. You know it. You are shocked at it. You don't enjoy it, but you are not brave enough to stand for modesty, for purity, for God. The fear of man has entangled you in a snare that has robbed you by making you compromise every bit of real power for Jesus Christ.

Silence and Inactivity

Again, the fear of man ensnares Christians into a guilty silence and inactivity. There are many of you who, when given the invitation to go to work and speak to the unsaved, want to do it. Oh, you would like to help someone come to Christ. What a joy it would be to you. But you say, "Suppose I talk to somebody, and he doesn't like it; suppose he laughs at me; suppose he says some hard things to me," and the fear of man—in your home, in your shop, in your hotel, everywhere you go—is shutting your mouth and robbing you of the transcendent joy of leading others to Jesus Christ. Well, friends, suppose others do laugh at you. They spat in your Master's face; they won't spit in yours. They struck Him with their fists; they probably won't strike you. They nailed Him to the cross. Are you not willing to be laughed at for a Master like that? I believe that the fear of man on the part of professed Christians, keeping them back from giving their testimony for Christ and from working to bring others to Christ, is doing far more to hinder the work of God than any other cause in our world today. Men are being saved by the thousands, but if you Christians would throw your fear to the winds and would have the boldness to witness and work for your Master on the streets, in the office, and in homes, they would be saved by the tens of thousands.

Rejection of Jesus

Again, the fear of man ensnares non-Christians into rejecting Jesus Christ. There are hundreds of men and women who would like to become Christians. They see the joy of it. They see that the Christian life is better than their current life, but they are afraid that if they accept Christ, somebody will ridicule them; and the fear of man is shutting them out of accepting Jesus Christ. I believe that more people are kept from accepting Christ by the fear of what someone will say or do than by any other cause. If we could get rid of this fear, I believe that five hundred or a thousand would be saved in a church service instead of two hundred or three hundred.

Shame in Confessing Christ

Again, the fear of man ensnares those who really think they have accepted Christ into not making a public confession of Christ. Jesus says distinctly, *"Whosoever therefore shall confess me before men, him will I confess also before my Father which is in heaven. But whosoever shall deny me before men, him will I also deny before my Father which is in heaven"* (Matthew 10:32–33). Paul says distinctly, *"With the heart man believeth unto righteousness; and with the mouth confession is made unto salvation"* (Romans 10:10). And yet a host of you men and women are trying to be Christians and never stand up to say so. You don't admit that it is the fear of man that keeps you from doing it. "Oh, no!" you say. "I don't believe in this publicity. I don't believe in this standing-up business. I believe in doing things more quietly. I don't believe in excitement." You give a thousand and one reasons, but, men, if you were honest with yourselves, as you will have to be honest with God some day, and told the truth, you would say, "It is because I am afraid to do it."

When we were in Edinburgh, a fine-looking young fellow came to me and said, "I am a cad." I said, "What is the matter?" He said, "I thought I accepted Christ here the other night, and I have not been man enough to tell another man in the office what I have done. I am a cad." Well, he was. So are you. You professed to take Jesus Christ. You told somebody so, quietly; but, to this day, you have not told the other men in your office, in your home, in your hotel, or in your shop. The fear of man has sealed your mouth and made you an arrant coward and robbed you of all the joy that there is in an out-and-out Christian experience.

Giving Up the Christian Life

Again, the fear of man ensnares those who start out in the Christian life from going on in it, perhaps because somebody says some discouraging thing. One night, when we were in a Scotch town, two young men both professed to accept Christ. The pastor of one of them sat on the platform. The new Christian went to his pastor and told him what he had done, and his pastor encouraged him. The other man's pastor was one of these convivial pastors, a man whose chief function is to serve as a figurehead at big feasts and encourage the fast men of the town by drinking their wine and joining in their tastes. If there is any man on earth for whom I am tempted to have utter contempt, it is a convivial minister, the minister whose chief function is to adorn big suppers and to drink rich men's wines. I would rather be a publican or a rum seller any day than a preacher of that kind. I have more respect for a good, straight-out rum seller than that kind of preacher. This man was that kind of a preacher. Occasionally, he had been seen on the streets when he needed the whole sidewalk. So, when this young man went to his preacher and told him what he had done, the preacher said, "Don't you believe a word they are saying up there." He discouraged him. Oh, the man that calls himself a minister of the gospel and dares to discourage a young convert in the first glimmerings of a new life. If there is a deeper spot in hell than any other, it is for the man who bears the name of minister and dares to discourage the young convert in his first aspirations toward God. Well, this man did, and the poor young fellow was discouraged quite entirely. Not excusable; still, a minister of the gospel had laughed at him and snared him into wretched backsliding, perhaps into hell. Oh, men and women starting out in the Christian life, no matter who approves or disapproves of your newfound faith, you are right. Go on, in spite of everybody.

Eternal Ruin

Again, the fear of man ensnares people to their eternal ruin. Oh, many men and women lie in Christless graves tonight, and will pass into a Christless eternity, because the fear of man kept them from accepting Christ.

When I am home in Chicago and have a night off, I often run out to another city to help ministers. One night, I ran across the line about twenty miles from Chicago, into the city of Hammond, Indiana. After speaking, I gave out the invitation, and among those who were moved by the Spirit of God was a young woman. She rose to her feet and started to come to the front. But the young man who sat beside her touched her arm. He was engaged to marry her. He said, "Don't go tonight. If you will wait for a few days, I may go with you." In fear of offending her fiancé, she sat down.

I went back the next week to speak in the opera house. At the close of the meeting, two young women came to me and said, "Oh,

Mr. Torrey, just as soon as you can get away from the opera house, come with us. There is a young lady who was going to go up to the front the other night, but the young man to whom she is engaged asked her to wait. She did wait, and now she has erysipelas (an acute febrile disease). It has gone to her brain, and she is dying. She probably won't live until morning. Come see her just as soon as you can get away from the opera house."

I hurried along from the opera house. I entered her home and went into the room where the poor girl lay dying, face all painted black with iodine, hardly recognizable as the same person, but perfectly conscious. I urged her then and there to take Christ. "No," she said. "I was about to start the last time you were here," and she told me the same story. "I didn't start then. I am dying; I can't start now."

I pled with her. I besought her. I knew it was her last hour. I did everything, but she would not yield; and when I passed out of that room of awful darkness, a young man in the hallway grasped me by the hand and took me into a cold, dark room; and though I could not see him, I could feel he was shaking like a leaf. "Oh," he said, "Mr. Torrey, I am engaged to marry that girl. When you spoke here last week, we were both at the meeting. When you gave out the invitation, she started for the front. I said, 'No, don't go; if you wait for me a few days, I may go with you.' She didn't go, and now she is dying without Christ. She is lost, and I am to blame. I am to blame."

Oh, men and women, the Spirit of God is moving with mighty power. Many of you are on the verge of a decision for Christ. Don't let the fear of man frighten you out of taking your stand.

Trusting in the Lord

The other part of the Scripture at the beginning of this chapter reads, "*Whoso putteth his trust in the* LORD *shall be safe"* (Proverbs 29:25). He will be safe from all danger of yielding to sin and temptation. If you trust God, temptation has no power over you. A man cannot yield to temptation without distrusting God. Every act of sin is an act of distrust in God. He who trusts God will do right, though the heavens fall.

I know a man in business in America. This man was unfortunate in business, lost about everything he had, and had to sell off everything in order to pay his honest debts. He kept from failing, he paid all his debts, but it left him practically penniless. Then an opening came for him as fireman on an engine. He came to me and said, "What shall I do? I have wanted to be an engine driver for years. They say they will promote me quickly, but if I take this post on a switch engine, I must work on the Sabbath. What shall I do?"

I said, "Well, you will have to decide for yourself; but if you can't do it with a clear conscience, you can't afford to do it." He said, "I can't do it with a clear conscience." He refused the position, though he did not know what he was to do to support himself and his wife and their family of three or four children. A day or two after that, he got a position at only a dollar a day—only four shillings—which is very low wages in America. In a few days, he got a position at $75 per month, and today he is head bookkeeper of one of the biggest mercantile establishments in the northwest, with a big salary, and he is constantly getting presents from the firm—all because he trusted God.

When I was home this summer, I found that there had been converted in my absence a young Jewish woman who was very brilliant and talented in the work that she had to do for a living to support her family. After she was converted, she was full of love for Christ, as Jews generally are when they are converted. She went out of the place where she worked, a very large establishment—all you businessmen would know the firm by name, if I should name it—and she commenced talking of Christ to the other employees.

Some of them did not like it, and they went to the head of the firm and said, "Miss So-and-so is constantly talking to us about Christ. We don't like it."

They called her in and said, "We have no objection to Christianity, no objection to your being a Christian. It is a good thing, but you must not talk it around this establishment."

"Very well," she said, "I won't work where I can't take Christ with me and talk for my Master." She had a family, an aged mother, and other members of the family to support, and she did not know where she was going—just converted from Judaism to Christianity.

"Well then," they said, "you will have to lose your position."

"Very well," she replied. "I will give up my position before I will be disloyal to Jesus Christ."

"Very well," they said. "Go back to your work."

She did just that. At the end of the week, she got a letter from the firm. She said, "Here is my discharge," and she tore it open. It read, "We have a place of very large responsibility, with a much larger salary than you are getting. We think you are the woman for the place, and we offer it to you." They saw she could be trusted. Businessmen are looking for men and women whom they can trust.

Again, whoso trusts in the Lord will be safe from danger of every kind. As we read in Romans 8:31, *"If God be for us, who can be against us?"* Oh, men will persecute you. Yes, they will ridicule you. They will do all they can to harm you. Jesus says in John 15:20, *"If they have persecuted me, they will also persecute you."* They will, but it won't do you any harm. Some people are frightened to death at being persecuted. Why, friends, it is one of the greatest privileges on earth for converts to be persecuted for Jesus Christ. Jesus says in Matthew 5:11–12, *"Blessed are ye, when men shall revile you, and persecute you, and shall say all manner of evil against you falsely, for* my sake. Rejoice"—not cry, not whine—"*and be exceeding glad: for great is your reward in heaven.*"

When we were in Ballarat, Australia, there was an organized gang that broke up our meeting. I had said some pretty plain things about dancing, like some I have said here, and I had been invited to go to a "decent dance." I went, and what I shared broke up the dance. They were ashamed to dance, and it broke up the club, and they never had but one dance after it. They regretted one invitation that they sent, anyhow. Well, the dancing elements were pretty badly excited. If I could stop several hundred of you society people from dancing, there would be a high time. I hope we have just such a high time. Well, this crowd that had organized to break up the meetings got away off in the far gallery. The very first night when they came there to break up the meetings, the power of God came down, and the two ringleaders walked right up from that rear gallery the whole length of the hall, came down to the front, turned round, and said, "We accept Jesus Christ."

The next day, some friends of one of the ringleaders met him on the street and knocked him down and pounded him to make him swear. But God had taken all the swearing out of him, and instead of swearing, he wrote one of the most beautiful letters I have ever seen in my life, about the joy of suffering for Jesus' sake— not to me, but to a friend of his, who sent it to me. Men, they may persecute you. They may pound you, and they may hound you, but they can't hurt you if you are right with God.

Once more, the man who trusts in the Lord is eternally safe. Jesus says in John 10:28–29:

> *I give unto them eternal life; and they shall never perish, nei- ther shall any man pluck them out of my hand. My Father, which gave them me, is greater than all; and no man is able to pluck them out of my Father's hand.*

If you trust in the Lord, the hand of God the almighty Father is underneath you and is round about you; the hand of Christ the Son is over you and round about you; and there you are, in between the almighty hand of God the Father and God the Son, and all the devils in hell can't get you.

Men, throw away your fear of man. In place of it, put trust in Jehovah. Compromising Christians, throw away your compromise. Be out-and-out for God—clean, straight Christians for God. Throw away your guilty silence. Go to work today to bring others to Christ, and keep it up tomorrow, and the next day and the next day. Throw away your guilty silence about unpopular truth, and declare the whole counsel of God, even though they say you are not up-to-date because you tell the truth. And, men and women who are rejecting Christ: Throw away your fear; fear not what anybody says, but stand up, accept Christ, and confess Him before the world.

In the early days of Mr. Moody's work in Chicago, there was a man in constant attendance at the services in the tabernacle. He seemed for a long time to be on the point of decision for Christ. At last, Mr. Moody went to him and urged him very strongly to decide at once. He replied that he could not come out as a Christian, that there was a man with whom he was associated who would ridicule him, and he could not endure his ridicule. Time after time, Mr. Moody urged upon him a decision, and the man at last became irritated and ceased attending the church.

Some months after, when the man had quite dropped out of sight, Mr. Moody received a very urgent call to go and see him at once. He found him very ill, apparently dying, and in great anxiety about his soul. He was shown the way of life, he professed to accept Christ, and his soul seemed at rest. To everyone's surprise, he took a turn for the better, and full recovery seemed sure. Mr. Moody called upon him and found him sitting outside in the sunshine.

"Now that you have accepted Christ," said Mr. Moody, "and God has raised you up, you will certainly come out at once and confess Him as soon as you are able to come to the tabernacle."

To Mr. Moody's astonishment, the man replied, "No, not now. I don't dare come out in Chicago, but I am intending soon to remove to Michigan; as soon as I get over there, I will come out publicly and take my stand on the side of Christ."

Mr. Moody told him that Christ could keep him in Chicago as well as in Michigan, but the man's fear of his friend held him back, and he refused to take his stand in Chicago. Mr. Moody left him, greatly disappointed. Just one week from that day, the man's wife called upon Mr. Moody and besought him to come at once and see her husband, for he had suffered a relapse and was worse than ever, and a council of physicians had agreed that there was no possibility of recovery.

"Did he send for me to come?" asked Mr. Moody.

"No," the wife replied, "he says that he is lost, that there is no hope for him. He does not wish to see you or to speak to you, but I cannot let him die in this way. You must come."

Mr. Moody hastened to the house and found the man in a state of utter despair. To all Mr. Moody's pleas for him to take Christ then and there, the man would reply that it was too late, that he was lost, that he had thrown away his day of opportunity, and that he could not be saved now.

Mr. Moody said, "I will pray for you."

"No," said the man, "don't pray for me. It is no use; I am lost. Pray for my wife and children. They need your prayers."

Mr. Moody knelt down by his side and prayed, but the heavens above his head seemed as brass. His own prayers did not seem to go higher than his head. He could not get hold of God for this man's salvation.

When he arose, the man said, "There, Mr. Moody, I knew that prayer would do no good; I am lost."

With a heavy heart, Mr. Moody left the house. All the afternoon, the man kept repeating, "'*The harvest is past, the summer is ended, and* [I am] *not saved*'" (Jeremiah 8:20). Just as the sun was setting behind the western prairies, the man passed away. In his last moment, they heard him whispering, and, leaning over to catch his words, they heard him murmuring, "'*The harvest is past, the summer is ended, and* [I am] *not saved*.'" Another soul went out into eternity unprepared, snared into eternal perdition by the fear of man.

Oh, men and women, I beseech of you, throw away your fear of man, put your trust in the Lord, and be saved.

13

HOW GOD LOVED THE WORLD

"For God so loved the world, that he gave his only begotten Son, that whosoever believeth in him should not perish, but have everlasting life."
—John 3:16

Go has given me for my text the verse of Scripture that, I suppose, has been used for the salvation of more people than any other verse in the Bible. It is John 3:16: *"For God so loved the world, that he gave his only begotten Son, that whosoever believeth in him should not perish, but have everlasting life."* Thousands of people have been saved by this wonderful verse—tens of thousands, hundreds of thousands—by simply reading it in the Bible, seeing it painted on the wall, or having it presented to them on a piece of cardboard.

If there were space, I could tell you of a boy who began to read through the Bible and was brought under very deep conviction of sin. As he read on and on, he came to the New Testament and to the gospel of John, where, in the third chapter, in the sixteenth verse, he read, *"For God so loved the world, that he gave his only begotten Son, that whosoever believeth in him should not perish, but have everlasting life."* And the moment he saw it, he saw Christ on the cross for his sins, and his burden all rolled away, and he found peace. I hope that hundreds will be converted through my text, whether they read this or not.

John 3:16 tells us some very important things about the love of God. It tells us that our salvation begins in God's love. We are not saved because we love God; we are saved because God loves us. Our salvation begins in God's loving us, and it ends in our loving God.

Universal Love

The first thing our Scripture teaches us about the love of God is that it is universal. *"God so loved the world"*—not some part of it, not some elect people, not some select class—but *"God so loved the world."* God loves the rich, but God loves the poor just as much as He loves the rich. If there should come to me one of the wealthiest men or women in Birmingham, and if, when I gave out the invitation, he or she should stand up and accept Christ, a great many of you people would be greatly pleased. So would I, for the rich need to hear the gospel just as much as the poor, and they are not nearly as likely to. But if some poor man should come to me, some man who has not a penny, some man who does not even know where he is going to sleep tonight, and if that man should stand up and take Christ, a good many of you would not think it amounted to much, but God would be just as pleased to see the poorest man or woman accept Christ as He would be to see the richest millionaire that there is in Birmingham.

God loves the educated, but He loves the uneducated just as much. God loves the great scholar, the man of science, the university professor, and the student, but He loves the man who can't read or write just as much as He loves the most brilliant scientist or philosopher that there is on earth. If some of your university professors should come, and should be converted, some of you people would be delighted. You would go out saying, "Oh, a wonderful thing happened. One of our learned professors came up there and was converted." But if some man or woman who can't even read or write should stand up and accept Christ, some of you people would not think it amounted to much. But God would be just as much pleased as He would be over the conversion of that university professor. The most wonderful thing of all about it is this that God loves the moral, the upright, the virtuous, and the righteous just as truly as He loves the sinner, the outcast, the abandoned, and the profligate. He loves the bad as He does the good.

One night, I was visiting one of the members of my church, and his little girl was playing around the room. The child did something naughty—I have since forgotten what it was—and her father called out, "Don't be naughty. If you are a good girl, God will love you, but if you are not, God won't love you."

I said, "Charlie, what nonsense are you teaching that child of yours? That is not what my Bible teaches. My Bible teaches that God loves the sinner just as truly as He loves the saint." And do you know, friends, it is so hard to make people believe this—that God does love the sinner, that God does love the outcast—that this is the truth the Bible emphasizes the most. For example, turn in your Bible to Romans 5:8: *"God commendeth his love toward us, in that, while we were yet sinners, Christ died for us."*

I was preaching in the city of Minneapolis on a hot summer's night, so hot that the windows in the building I was in were all open to let a little fresh air in, and the room was packed. At the back end of the room, a man was sitting where the window frame had been taken out; and when I gave out the invitation for all who wished to be saved that night to hold up their hands, that man sitting in the window raised his hand. But as soon as I pronounced the benediction, that man started for the door. I forgot all about my after-meeting. I don't know to this day what became of that after-meeting. All I saw was that man starting for the door, and I started after him. I caught him just as he turned to descend the stairway. I laid my hand upon his shoulder just as he turned the corner. I said to him, "My friend, you held up your hand to say you wanted to be saved."

"Yes, I did," he said.

"Why didn't you stay, then, to the second meeting?"

He responded, "It is no use."

"Why?" I asked. "God loves you."

He replied, "You don't know who you are talking to."

I said, "I don't care who I am talking to. I know God loves you."

"I am the meanest thief in Minneapolis."

"Well," I responded, "if you are the meanest thief in Minneapolis, I can prove to you from the Bible that God loves you." I opened my Bible to Romans 5:8 and read aloud, "'*God commendeth his love toward us, in that, while we were yet sinners, Christ died for us.*' Now," I said, "if you are the meanest thief in Minneapolis, you are certainly a sinner, and that verse says that God loves sinners."

It broke the man's heart, and he commenced to weep. I took him to my office with me, and we sat down so he could tell me his story. He said, "I am just out of confinement. I was released from prison this morning. I had started out this evening, with some companions whom I knew, to commit one of the most daring burglaries that was ever committed in this city; and by tomorrow morning, I would have had either a big stake of money or a bullet in my body. But as we were going down the street together, we passed the corner where you were holding that open-air meeting. You had a Scotchman speaking. My mother was a Scotchwoman, and when I heard that Scotch tongue, it reminded me of my mother. I had a dream about my mother the other night in prison. I dreamed that she came to me and begged me to give up my wicked life; and when I heard that Scotchman talk, I stepped up to listen. My two pals said, 'Come along,' and cursed me. I said, 'I am going to listen to what this man says.' Then they tried to drag me across the street, but I would not go. What that man said touched my heart, and when you gave out the invitation to the meeting, I came, and that is why I am here."

I opened my Bible, and I showed that man that God loves sinners, that Christ had died for sinners, and how he could be saved by simply accepting Christ right then and there. And he did accept Christ. We knelt down, side by side, and that man offered up one of the most wonderful prayers I had ever heard in all my life.

Are you a thief? God loves you. Are you a pickpocket? God loves you. Are you a lost woman? God loves you. Are you an atheist? God loves you. Are you a blasphemer? God loves you. I will tell you something you can't find in all the world. You can't find in all the world a man or woman that God doesn't love.

Holy Love

The second thing our text teaches us about the love of God is that God's love is a holy love. "God *so* loved the world, that he *gave his only begotten Son*" (Romans 5:8). A great many people cannot understand that. They say, "I cannot see why God loves me if He doesn't forgive my sins outright without His Son dying in my place. I cannot see the necessity of Christ's death. If God is love, and if God loves me and loves everybody, why doesn't He take us to heaven right away without Christ's having to die for us?"

The text answers the question: "*God so loved.*" That "*so*" brings out the character of God's love. It was of such a character that God could not and would not pardon sin without an atonement. God is a holy God. God's love is a holy love. Now, God's holiness, like everything in God, is real. There is no hypocrisy in God. It is real love, real righteousness, and real holiness; and God's holiness, since it is real, must manifest itself in some way. It must either manifest itself in the punishment of the sinner—that is, in our eternal banishment from Him, in your ruin and in mine—or it must manifest itself in some other way.

Now, the atoning death of Jesus Christ upon the cross of Calvary was God substituting His atoning action, whereby He expressed His hatred of sin, for His punitive action, whereby He would have expressed the same thing. But some man says, "That is not just. The doctrine you teach is this—God, the first Person, took the sin of man, the second person, and laid it upon Jesus Christ, an innocent third Person. That is not just." Well, that would not be just; but that is not what the Bible teaches, and that is not what I teach. I don't teach, and the Bible doesn't teach, that God, a holy first Person, will take the sins of you and me, guilty second persons, and lay them upon Jesus Christ, an innocent third Person. Jesus Christ was not a third Person. "*God was in Christ, reconciling the world unto himself*" (2 Corinthians 5:19), and the atoning death of Jesus Christ on the cross is not God taking my sin and laying it on a third person; it is God the Father taking the penalty of my sin

How God Loved the World 181

into His own heart and dying in His Son, in whom He personally dwelt, in place of the rebel.

Again, Jesus Christ was not merely the first Person; He was the second Person, too. Jesus Christ was the Son of Man, the second Adam, the representative man. No ordinary man could have died for you and me. It would have been of no value. But Jesus Christ was the second Adam, the second head of the race, the second Person, your representative and mine. When Christ died on the cross of Calvary, I died in Him, and the penalty of my sin was paid.

Friends, the philosophy of the atonement, as laid down in the Bible, is the most profound and wonderful philosophy the world has ever seen or heard. The Christian doctrine is a perfect whole. Take out one doctrine, and the others are irrational; but put them all together, and they are a perfect system. For example, if you become a Unitarian and take out the deity of Christ, the atonement becomes irrational. If you take the humanity out of Christ and are left with Jesus Christ merely divine, the atonement becomes irrational. But if you take all that the Bible says—that God was in Christ, and that in Christ the Word became flesh, real man, God manifest in the flesh—then the atonement of Christ is the most profoundly and wonderfully philosophical truth the world has ever seen!

God's love was a holy love. I thank God that it was. I thank God that His method was such that, in perfect righteousness, perfect justice, and perfect holiness, as well as in perfect love, on the ground of Christ's atoning death, He could pardon and save the vilest of sinners. And, men and women, when you are awakened to a proper sense of your sinfulness—when you see yourselves as you really are—and when you see God as He really is, nothing will satisfy your conscience but the doctrine that God, the Holy One, substituted His atoning action, whereby He expressed His hatred of sin, for His punitive action, whereby He would have expressed the same thing, that in the death of Jesus Christ on the cross of Calvary, your sin and mine were perfectly settled forever.

Thank God, the broken law of God has no claim upon me. I broke it, I admit; but Jesus Christ kept it, and, having kept it, He satisfied its punitive claim by dying for those who had not kept it. On the ground of that atoning death, there is pardon for the vilest sinner. A man says, "There is no forgiveness for me." Why not? "Because I have gone down so deep in sin." Listen, men: You have gone down deep into sin; you have gone deeper into sin than you realize yourself; but while your sins are as high as the mountains, the atonement that covers them is as high as heaven. While your sins are as deep as the ocean, the atonement that swallows them up is as deep as eternity; and on the ground of Christ's atoning death, there is pardon tonight for the vilest sinner in your city, for the vilest sinner on the face of this earth.

Great Love

The third thing our Scripture teaches us about the love of God is the greatness of that love. *"For God so loved the world, that he gave his only begotten Son, that whosoever believeth in him should not perish, but have everlasting life."* The greatness of God's love comes out in two ways in the text: first of all, in the greatness of the gift He offers us—eternal life. It does not mean merely a life that is endless in its duration. Thank God, it means that; but it means more. It means a life that is perfect and divine in its quality, as well as endless in its duration, and that is what is offered to you. *"For God so loved the world, that he gave his only begotten Son, that whosoever believeth in him should not perish, but have **everlasting life**."*

I do thank God for a life that is perfect in quality and that will never end. Most of us have got to die before long, as far as our physical life is concerned. A large number of the people I preach to will be in their graves in a few months, more of us in a year, more in five, still more in ten, almost all of us in forty. Eighty years from now, probably, there won't be a person whom I preach to on this earth, unless the Lord has come before. "Well," you say, "eighty years is a pretty long time." No, it is not. It looks long to you young people. It looks long to look forward to, but when you get to be forty-eight, as I am, and there are only thirty-two years of it left, it does not look very long. It looks very short. Eighty years don't look very long; and, friends, when the eighty years are up, what then?

Suppose I had a guarantee that I was going to live two hundred years in perfect health, strength, and prosperity. Would that satisfy me? No, it would not. For when the two hundred years are up, what then? Suppose I had a guarantee that I was to live a thousand years in perfect health and strength and prosperity. Would that satisfy me? No, it would not. For when the thousand years are up, what then? Suppose I had a guarantee that I should live on this earth for ten thousand years in perfect health and strength and prosperity. Would that satisfy me? No, it would not. For when the ten thousand are up, what then? Men, I want something that never ends; and, thank God, I have got something that never ends in Christ. Thousands of years will pass into tens of thousands, tens of thousands will pass into millions, millions will pass into hundreds of millions, hundreds of millions will pass into billions, and the billions will pass into trillions, and I will be living on and on and on in ever-growing joy and glory. Eternal life! Eternal life! And who can have it? Anybody. *"Whosoever believeth in him."*

What does *"whosoever"* mean? Somebody once asked a little boy, "What does 'whosoever' mean?" and the little fellow answered, "It means you and me and everybody else." Thank God, it does. It means you and me and everybody else. Somebody once said—I think it was John Bradford—that he was glad that John 3:16 did not read, "God so loved the world, that He gave His only begotten

Son, that John Bradford might have everlasting life; for if it read that way, I would be afraid it meant some other John Bradford. But when I read that '*God so loved the world, that he gave his only begotten Son, that **whosoever** believeth in him,*' I know that means me." Thank God it did, and it means everybody else who is reading this.

Friends, I came with a pocket pretty well filled with shillings, half crowns, gold coins, checks, and so on, that came to me through the mail today. They are all gone. I handed them all over to the treasurer. But tonight, while I go out with an empty pocket, I will go out with a full heart—a heart that is full of everlasting life—and that is worth millions of gold coins. Every other man and woman can go out the same way.

But the text tells us a second way, more wonderful yet, in which the greatness of the love of God shows itself, and that is in the sacrifice that God made for us. "*God so loved the world, that he gave his only begotten Son.*" Now, as I have said before, the measure of love is sacrifice. You can tell just how much anybody loves you by the sacrifice that he is willing to make for you. God has shown the measure of His love by the sacrifice He made. What was it? His very best. He "*so loved the world, that he gave his only begotten Son,*" the dearest that He had. No earthly father ever loved his son as God loved Jesus Christ. I have an only son; how I love him! We have oftentimes wished that God, in His kindness, had given us three or four sons, provided they were all like the one He gave us, just as He has given us four daughters; but I was thinking of it this afternoon, and this thought occurred to me—that perhaps the reason why God had given us only one son was that I might have a little deeper realization of how much God loved Jesus Christ.

Friends, suppose someday I should see that boy of mine arrested. Suppose he went as a missionary to China, and I went as missionary to China, and I saw him arrested by the enemies of Christ. Suppose they blindfolded him, spat on him, punched him in his face, plaited a crown of great big cruel thorns, and put it on his brow; and then some Chinaman comes along and, with a heavy stick, knocks that crown down upon his brow until the blood pours down his face on either side. How do you suppose I would feel? Then suppose they stripped off his garments, took him and bound him to a post, and made him lean over until the skin of his back was drawn taut; then a soldier came along with a long stick with long lashes of leather in which were twisted bits of brass and lead. The soldier laid the lash upon my son's back thirty-nine times, till it was all torn and bleeding, and he was one mass of bloody wounds. How do you think I would feel?

Then suppose they laid a cross down upon the ground and stretched his right hand out on the arm of the cross, put a nail in the hand, lifted a heavy hammer, and drove the nail through his hand; then they stretched his left arm on the other arm of the cross, put a nail in the palm of that hand, and lifted the heavy hammer and sent the nail through that hand. Then they put a nail through his feet, lifted the heavy hammer, and drove the nail through his feet. Then they took that cross to which he was nailed and plunged it into a hole on the rock, leaving him hanging there, his agony getting worse and worse every minute. Seeing him hanging there beneath the burning sun from nine o'clock in the morning till three o'clock in the afternoon, standing and looking on as my only boy dies in awful agony on a cross, how do you suppose I would feel?

But, men, that is just what God saw. He loved His only begotten Son as you and I never dreamt of loving our sons. He saw His persecutors spit in His face; He saw them blindfold Him; He saw them smite Him with their fists; He saw them take rods and beat Him; He saw them take the crown of awful thorns and press it on His brow, then smite it down with a heavy rod; He saw them strip the garments off His back, tie Him to a post, make Him lean over until the skin upon His back was drawn taut; then He saw a brawny Roman soldier take that awful scourge with long leather lashes, into which were twisted bits of brass and lead, and lay it on His back thirty-nine times, till it made Jesus one mass of aching wounds. He saw them take Him and stretch Him on a cross, drive a nail into both of His hands, drive a nail through both of His feet, and take that cross and plunge it into a hole on that rock, leaving Him hanging there, aching, all His bones out of joint, tortured in every member of His body! God looked on. Why did He suffer it? Because He loved you and me, and it was the only way that you and I could be saved. *"God so loved the world, that he gave his only begotten Son, that whosoever believeth on him should not perish, but have everlasting life"* (John 3:16).

Men, how are you going to repay that love today? I know how some of you are going to repay it. You are going to repay it with hatred. You hate God. You never said it, but it is true.

A friend of mine was preaching one time in Connecticut. He was stopping with a physician who had a beautiful, amiable daughter. She had never made a profession of religion, but she was such a beautiful character that people thought she was a Christian. One night, after the meetings had been going on for some time, my friend asked this young lady, "Are you going up to the meeting tonight?"

She answered, "No, Mr. Hammond, I am not."

"Oh," he said, "I think you had better go."

She replied, "I will not go."

"Why?" he inquired. "Don't you love God?"

"I hate God," she responded. She had never realized it before. I think she would have said she loved God up to that time, but when the demands of God were pressed home by the Holy Spirit, she was not willing to obey, and she found out that she hated God.

Some of you have never found out that you hate God, but it is true. How some of you use the name of God today! You have used it many times. In prayer? No, in profanity. Why? Because you hate God.

Some of you men, if your wives should take Christ, you would make life unendurable. Why? Because you hate God, and you are going to make your wife miserable for accepting His Son.

Some of you young people, if some other young person in your office or your factory or your workplace should accept Christ, you would laugh at him for it. Why? Because you hate God.

Some of you people will read every infidel book you can get, and will go to every infidel lecture. You are trying to convince yourself that the Bible is not God's Word; and if anybody would come along and bring up some smart objection to the Bible, you would laugh at it and rejoice in it. Why? Because you hate God, and you want to get rid of God's Book.

Some of you men and women just love to hold up your heads and say, "I don't believe in the divinity of Christ; I don't believe He is the Son of God." Why? Because you hate God, and if you can rob His divine Son of the honor that belongs to Him, you will do it. You are repaying the wondrous love of God with hatred.

Some of you are refusing to accept Christ. When people speak to you, you get angry. You say, "I wish you would not talk to me. Go about your own business. It is none of your business whether I am a Christian or not." You get angry every time anybody speaks to you. Why? Because you hate God.

Some of you so bitterly hate God that you are trying to find fault with the doctrine of the atonement. You are trying to make yourself believe that Christ did not die on the cross for you. You say, "I cannot understand the philosophy of it." If you loved God, you would not stop to ask the philosophy of it. You would simply lift your heart in simple gratitude and praise to God for so loving you that He gave His Son to die for you.

Conquering Love

There is one other thing that our text teaches us about the love of God, and that is the conquering power of God's love. *"For God so loved the world, that he gave his only begotten Son, that whosoever believeth in him should not perish, but have everlasting life"* (John 3:16). The love of God conquers sin; the love of God conquers death; the love of God conquers wrong and saves men from perishing unto everlasting life. And, men and women, the love of God conquers where everything else fails.

The first time I ever preached in Chicago—it was several years before I went there to live—after the sermon, among the people who stood up that night to say they wanted to be prayed for, I noticed a young woman who did not come forward with the rest. I went down to where she was standing and urged her to come forward. She laughed and said, "No, I am not going forward," and she sat down again.

The following night was not an evangelistic service but a meeting of the convention. I was president of the convention. As I looked over the audience, I saw that young woman toward the back in the audience, elegantly dressed—the most finely dressed woman in the audience. I called somebody else to the chair and slipped around to the back part of the building. When the meeting was dismissed, I made my way to where that young lady was sitting. I sat down beside her and asked, "Won't you take Christ tonight?"

"No," she replied. "Would you like to know the kind of life I am living?" It was not known that she was living that kind of life. She was living it in the best society, honored and respected. Then she commenced to unfold to me one of the saddest stories of dishonor I have ever listened to, without blushing or laughing as if it were a good joke. Finally, she said, "Let me tell you how I spent last Easter."

I cannot tell you how it was—how any woman of any sense could have told it to any man—and when she had finished the story, she burst out into a laugh and said, "That was a funny way to spend Easter, wasn't it?"

I was dumbfounded. I simply took my Bible—I had a little Bible with fine print—and opened it to John 3:16, passed it over to her, and said, "Won't you please read that?" She had to hold it very near to her eyes to see the print, and she commenced in a laughing way. "'*God so loved*'"—she was laughing no more—"'*the world*'"—there was nothing like a laugh now—"'*that he gave his only begotten Son.*'" She burst into tears, and the tears literally flowed down onto the elegant silk robe that she was wearing. Hardened as she was, brazen as she was, shameless as she was, trifling as she was, one glimpse of Jesus on the cross of Calvary had broken her heart. God grant that it may break yours, as well.

I want to tell you one more incident. One night, I was preaching, and we had an after-meeting. The leading soprano in my choir was not a Christian. I don't believe in having an unconverted choir; therefore, we don't allow anybody in our choir who is not a saved person, to the best of our knowledge. You say, "You must have a pretty small choir." We have two hundred, and every one of them, as far as we know, is a believer. But in that church, it was not so, and my leading soprano was not a Christian. She was a happy, worldly girl, not immoral at all and a very respectable girl, but very happy and very worldly.

She stayed for the after-meeting. Down in the body of the house, her mother arose and said, "I wish you would all pray for the conversion of my daughter." I did not look round at the choir, but I knew perfectly well how that young woman appeared. I knew her cheeks were burning, I knew her eyes were flashing, and I knew that she was angry from the crown of her head to the soles of her feet. Just as soon as the meeting was over, I hurried down to the particular door that I knew she would have to pass out by. As she came along, I advanced toward her, held out my hand, and said, "Good evening, Cora."

Her eyes flashed, and her cheeks burned. She did not take my hand. She stamped her foot and said, "Mr. Torrey, my mother knows better than to do what she has done tonight. She knows it will only make me worse."

I said, "Cora, sit down."

The angry girl sat down, and I opened my Bible to Isaiah 53:5, then handed it to her. I said, "Won't you please read it?"

She read, "'*He was wounded for our transgressions, he was bruised for our iniquities: the chastisement of our peace was upon him.*'" She did not get any further; she burst into tears. The love of God, revealed in the cross of Christ, had broken her heart. I left the city the next day. While I was away, I got a letter saying that this young lady was happily converted but very ill. I returned to Minneapolis, called her house, and found that she was rejoicing in Christ but so ill that the physician held out no hope of her recovery.

A few days after, her brother came running up to my house about ten o'clock in the morning. He said, "Mr. Torrey, come down to the house as quick as you can. Cora has been unconscious all the morning. She has not spoken a word. She hardly seems to be breathing. She is as white as marble, and we think she is dying. She seems to be utterly unconscious."

I hurried down there. And there lay the whitest living person I had ever seen, bleeding to death through her gums and nose. She was apparently perfectly unconscious and had not said a word all the morning.

Her mother stood at the foot of the bed with a breaking heart. "Oh," she said, "Mr. Torrey, pray, pray, please pray!" I knelt down by the bedside and prayed. I didn't suppose the girl would hear a word I said. I was praying to comfort her mother. And just as soon as I had finished my prayer, there came from those white lips—in a clear, strong, full, beautiful voice—the most wonderful prayer I have ever heard in my life.

The dying girl said, "Oh, heavenly Father, I want to live, if it be Thy will, so that, as I have sung in the past for my own glory, I can sing for the glory of Jesus, who loved me and gave Himself for me. Father, I want to live; but if Thou dost not see fit to raise me up from this bed, I shall be glad to depart and be with Christ." And she departed to be with Christ. The love of God had conquered.

Men and women, let the love of God conquer your stubborn, wicked, foolish, sinful, worldly, careless hearts. "*God so loved the world, that he gave his only begotten Son, that whosoever believeth in him should not perish, but have everlasting life*" (John 3:16). Yield to that love today. Amen.

14

TODAY AND TOMORROW

"The Holy Ghost saith, To day."
—Hebrews 3:7

"Boast not thyself of to morrow."
—Proverbs 27:1

Today is the wise man's day; tomorrow is the fool's day. The wise man is the man who, when he sees what ought to be done, does it today. The foolish man is the man who, when he sees what ought to be done, says, "I will do it tomorrow." The men who always do today the thing that ought to be done today are the men who make a success for time and for eternity. The men who put off until tomorrow what ought to be done today are the men who make a shipwreck of time and eternity. *"The Holy Ghost saith, To day"* (Hebrews 3:7). Man, in the folly of his heart, says, "Tomorrow."

I am going to give you five reasons why every truly wise man who has not already accepted Christ as his Savior, surrendered to Him as his Lord and Master, and openly confessed Him as such before the world, should do it now. I have no doubt that there are literally hundreds, if not thousands, of men and women who intend to be Christians sometime, but who keep saying, "Not yet," "Not today." Now I am going to tell you not merely why you ought to become Christians but why you ought to become Christians today.

Find Wonderful Joy

First, the sooner you come to Christ, the sooner you will find the wonderful joy that is to be found in Him. It admits of no controversy that there is, in Jesus Christ, an immeasurably better joy than there is in the world; a purer joy, a higher joy, a holier joy, a more satisfying joy, a more abiding joy, a joy more wonderful in every way. This fact does not admit of dispute. Everyone who keeps his eyes open knows that it is true. Go to any person who has ever tried the world and tried Christ, and put to him the question "Which joy is better—the joy you have found in the world or the joy you have found in Christ?" You will get the same answer every time.

The joy found in the world is not for a moment to be compared with the joy that is found in Christ. I have tried both. I have had abundant opportunity to try both. If ever a person had an opportunity to try what this world can give, I had it, and I tried it. I tried all that could be found in the world. Then I turned to Christ and tried Him, and my testimony is just like the testimony of millions of others who have found that the joy in the world is nothing and the joy in Christ is everything. I don't care how fully a person may have gone into the joys of this world, or how great his opportunity may have been to test them; every man who has tried both and has really found Christ will tell you that joy in Christ is higher, deeper, broader, wider, longer, and more wonderful in every way than the joy that the world gives. Well, friends, the sooner you come to Christ, the sooner you will have that joy.

Escape Wretchedness and Misery

Second, the sooner you come to Christ, the sooner you will escape the wretchedness and misery that there are away from Christ. First of all, there is the misery of an accusing conscience. No one out of Christ has peace of conscience.

One night, I was preaching to an audience of men and women to whom twenty dollars would have been a great help. I put my hand in my pocket as I was preaching, and I felt the twenty dollars I had in there. I took it out, held it up, and said, "Now, if there is a man in this audience out of Christ who has peace in his heart— deep, abiding satisfaction and rest—and will come up here and say so, I will give him this twenty dollars." Nobody came up.

When the meeting was over, I went down and stood at the door with the twenty dollars, for I thought they might be timid about coming up for it. I said, "If anybody can claim this twenty dollars on the conditions I have named, who can say, 'I have peace of conscience and heart; my heart is satisfied without Christ,' he can have the twenty dollars." They commenced to file out, but nobody claimed it. Finally, a man came along, and I asked him, "Don't you want this twenty dollars?"

"But I cannot claim it on those conditions," he said.

Neither can you.

Another night, I was preaching in Chicago, and I asked every-body in the building who had found rest and perfect satisfaction through the acceptance of Christ to stand up. Hundreds of men and women, more than a thousand, rose to their feet. Then I asked them to sit down and said, "If there is an infidel in this house who can say he has found rest and peace and perfect satisfaction of heart in infidelity, will he please stand?"

There were a lot of infidels there. I saw one man stand up in the gallery, and I said, "I see there is a gentleman up there. I am glad that he has the courage of his convictions. I would like to speak with him in the after-meeting."

He came to the after-meeting. I said, "Mr. S—, you stood up in the meeting tonight to say that you had perfect rest and peace of heart without Christ, and that your soul was satisfied in infidelity. Is that true?"

"Oh," he said, "Mr. Torrey, that will have to be qualified."

I guess it will. There is no peace, saith my God, for the wicked. (See Isaiah 48:22; 57:21.)

Then there is the slavery of sin away from Christ. "*Whosoever committeth sin is the servant of sin*" (John 8:34). Away from Christ is apprehension of what may happen, apprehension of disaster, apprehension of what man may do, apprehension of what may lie beyond the grave. Men and women, when you really come to Christ, you are freed from the fear of man; you have no fear of misfortune, for you are able to say, "*All things work together for good to them that love God*" (Romans 8:28); you have no fear of death, for what men call death is simply to depart and be with Christ. The moment you really accept Christ, you get rid of all this wretchedness, you get rid of the accusations of conscience, you get rid of the slavery of sin, you get rid of all apprehensions of disaster, you get rid of the dread of death. Why not get rid of it all right now?

Suppose you were on the shore on a cold, wintry night and saw in the distance a wreck and a man clinging to the wreck, and, every once in a while, the cold waters would sweep over him. You and others would go out in a lifeboat and would say to him, "We have come to take you off. Drop into the lifeboat." But suppose the man would say, "No, I think I can hold on until morning; come out again in the morning, and I will get into the boat and come ashore." You would say to him, "Man, are you mad? Stay out here tonight when you can come ashore now?"

Oh, men and women, you are out hanging on the wreck, and, every little while, the cold waves break over you—all the wretchedness of an accusing conscience, all the wretchedness of the bondage of sin, all the wretchedness of the fear of possible death, all the multiplied wretchedness of the soul away from God. Why cling to the wreck another night when you can come ashore to safety and joy now, if you will but drop right into the lifeboat?

Do More for Christ

Third, the sooner you come to Christ, the more you can do for Christ. The moment a person is saved, he wants to do something for the Master. If you are saved a year from today, you will go to work for Christ, but there will be one year gone that you can never get back. Today, you are associated with friends whom you can lead to Christ; a year from now, they may be past your reach.

Before I was converted, I had a friend, and we were often together. We lived in the same building, and we went pleasuring together. If I had been a Christian, I could have led him to Christ. Three years later, after I had accepted Christ, that young man passed beyond my reach.

The day I went back to the university to study for my second degree, my father picked up the New York Herald and began to read about a young man who was out playing ball. The man out in the center field threw the ball in. This young man's back was toward the center field, and he was struck at the base of his brain and never regained his consciousness. As my father read this and came to the name, he said, "Archie, is not that your old friend?"

I took up the paper, read it, and said, "Yes, it is my old friend." Called into eternity without a moment's warning, and my opportunity of bringing him to Christ gone forever! Oh, in the years that have come since, God has used me to lead others to Christ; and how often I have thought back of Frank. In spite of all those who are now coming to Christ, Frank is gone, and my opportunity of saving him is lost forever. Men and women, you postpone taking Christ for thirty days, and people whom you might have reached during that time will have passed beyond your reach forever.

In my first pastorate, a woman a little over fifty years of age who had been a backslider was saved through and through, and she became the best worker in all the community; but her own two sons had grown up during the years that she was far away from God. They had both married and passed beyond her reach, and though she has been used to bring so many people to Christ, she has never been able to bring her two sons to Christ. The day of opportunity for them was while she was living in the world.

Fathers and mothers, if you are not saved today, you may be some other day; but your sons and daughters, who might join you if you come today, will very likely have passed beyond your reach forever if you wait too long. The sooner you come to Christ, the more people you can bring with you, so come today.

Reap Treasures in Eternity

Fourth, the sooner you come to Christ, the richer will be your eternity. We are saved by grace; we are rewarded according to our works. Every day of a man's life after he is saved, he is laying up treasures in heaven; and every day you live for Christ, you will be that much richer for eternity. Now, some people have an idea that a man can be saved on his deathbed and have just as abundant an entrance into the kingdom of God as a man who had been saved forty years could have. Oh, what nonsense! You have neither common sense nor Bible for it. A man may be saved on his deathbed. I don't say that no man ever is; I believe some are, though not very many. A man may be saved on his deathbed, but he is saved *"so as by fire"* (1 Corinthians 3:15). His works are all burned up, and he enters heaven penniless. The man who is saved forty years before he dies, and serves Christ for forty years, every day of these forty years he is making his deposits in eternity, for which he will be richer throughout all eternity. *"Lay up for yourselves treasures in heaven."* (Matthew 6:20).

Oh, men and women, the sooner you come to Christ, with so much fuller hands can you enter the kingdom of God. I do thank God I was converted when I was, but what would I give for those six wasted years through which I deliberately resisted the Spirit of God! But I can't call them back.

Be Sure of Your Salvation

Fifth, the sooner you come to Christ, the surer you are to come to Christ. If you are not saved today, you may be tomorrow, but you may not. I believe there are scores of people who will be saved today or never. When a person stands on a platform and looks over a vast audience, feeling in his very soul that the eternal salvation of hundreds of souls is trembling in the balances as the result of that sermon, it is an awful feeling; but that is the feeling I have now. I believe there are hundreds of people who will read this and will either be saved right now or never. The Spirit of God may leave you. People think they can turn to Christ when they will, but, men and women, when the Spirit of God is in the room, passing from seat to seat and from heart to heart, it is an awful moment. To say yes means life; to say no means death. To say yes means heaven; to say no means hell. Oftentimes, a man will be so near the kingdom, and he will say, "I am so interested, I will certainly be just as much interested tomorrow"; but the critical hour has come, and if you do not yield today, you will have no interest tomorrow.

I once received a message from a wealthy young fellow in New Haven, Connecticut, saying that he wished to see me that night at Mr. Moody's meeting. I went and met him at the close of the meeting. He was on the verge of a decision. As we stood talking on Chapel Street, opposite the college, the college bell rang out a late hour. I said to myself, *He is so near a decision, I can leave him safely until tomorrow morning.* So, I said, "Good night, Will. I will be around to your room tomorrow morning at ten." It was one of the most fatal mistakes I ever made. I was there at ten, but he was not—his convictions had all left him. He was as hard as flint. His opportunity had come and gone. Oh, men and women, you may be very near a decision tonight, on the very borders of the kingdom; but if you say no today, tomorrow will be forever too late.

Then, again, who of us can tell in a moment who will be called out of the world into eternity? At our first men's meeting in the Empire Theatre in Edinburgh, a Roman Catholic young man accepted Christ. Little did he or we realize that this was his last chance. The next day, he was hurried to the hospital for an operation, and the operation proved fatal. By accepting Christ at that meeting, he was just in time. If he had waited a day, he would have been lost forever.

Men and women, you have a chance today.

Don't throw it away. The sooner you take Christ, the surer you will be to take Him. Take Him now. You can have the joy of salvation today; why wait a week? You can be saved from a life of wretchedness today. Why stand it another week? The sooner you come to Christ, the more you can do for Christ. Why not come to Him? The sooner you come to Christ, the richer you will be throughout all eternity. Why not come to Him and begin to lay up treasures in the bank of heaven? (See Matthew 6:20.) The sooner you come to Christ, the surer it is that you will come. Come now. *"The Holy Ghost saith, To day"* (Hebrews 3:7). *"Boast not thyself of to morrow; for thou knowest not what a day may bring forth"* (Proverbs 27:1).

"HE THAT WINNETH SOULS IS WISE"

"He that winneth souls is wise."
—Proverbs 11:30

If I should go up and down the streets of Birmingham and ask the different men and women whom I meet, "Whom do you regard as the wise man?" I would get a great variety of answers. I might go, for example, into some of the banks and ask the man in charge, "Whom do you regard as the wise man?" Very likely, I would get an answer like, "I regard the man who succeeds in getting the most money as the wise man—the man who, by virtue of rare business sagacity and unusual industry, amasses a fortune of first a thousand pounds and then ten thousand pounds and then a hundred thousand pounds and then a million pounds and then two, three, four, five, ten, million pounds—I regard him as the wise man."

If I should go into a political office, I would get a different answer. Very likely, the man would reply, "I regard the man who studies the economic and political problems of the day until he has mastered them, who succeeds in finding out what is best for his country's financial welfare, who wins the confidence of his fellow citizens, and so is elected to Parliament and is afterward made a cabinet minister and then prime minister—I regard him as the wise man."

If I should go to your military men, I would get a different answer still. Very likely, the reply would be something like this: "I regard the man who masters the art of war, who studies the science of tactics and maneuvers until he knows how to maneuver great forces on the field of battle, to lead them on to victory; the man who first becomes a captain, then a major, then a lieutenant colonel, then a colonel, then a brigadier general, then a major general, then a lieutenant general, and finally a field marshal—I regard him as the wise man."

If I should go to your young men and women, I would get a different answer. Very likely, they would say to me, "I regard the man or woman who gets the most pleasure out of life, who finds the most fun by day and the most amusement by night—I regard him as the wise man."

But when I turn away from men, with all these discordant answers, and look up to God and ask, "Heavenly Father, whom dost Thou regard as the wise man?" there comes thundering down from yonder throne of eternal light this answer: *"He that winneth souls is wise"* (Proverbs 11:30). Not he that wins money, not he that wins political distinctions and honor and position, not he that wins renown in the field of battle, not he that wins the most sport and amusement in life, but he that wins the most men and women to a saving knowledge of Jesus Christ—he is the wise man.

Men and women, in the eyes of God, the wise man is the man who makes soulwinning the business of his life; and my main proposition is this: that every follower of Jesus Christ should make the winning of others to Christ the business of his life. I know that some of you say, "I don't believe that; I believe that the statement is altogether too strong." I am going to give you six unanswerable reasons why soulwinning should be the business of life on the part of every follower of Jesus Christ.

It Is What We Are Commanded to Do

First of all, soulwinning should be the business of life with every Christian because it is the work that Jesus Christ has commanded us to do. When the Lord Jesus Christ left this earth, He left His marching orders to the church. You will find them in Matthew 28:19: *"Go ye therefore, and teach all nations."* That commandment was not merely for the first twelve disciples; it was for every follower of Jesus Christ in every age of the church's history. If you will read the book of Acts, you will see very plainly that in the early church, every Christian considered that the Great Commission—to make disciples, to win souls—was for himself. For example, if you turn to Acts 8:4, you will read these words: *"They that were scattered abroad went every where preaching the word"*; and these that were scattered abroad were not the apostles but the rank and file, the ordinary, everyday members of the church.

Some years ago, when I was speaking in the city of Minneapolis in America, I noticed in the audience a young lawyer. When the meeting was over, I made my way to him and asked him, "Are you a Christian?"

"Well, sir," he said, "I consider myself a Christian."

I said, "Are you bringing other men to Christ?"

He responded, "No, I am not. That is not my business; that's your business. I am not called to do that. I am called to practice law; you are called to preach the gospel."

I said, "If you are called to be a Christian, you are called to bring other men to Christ."

He replied, "I don't believe it."

"Look here." Then I opened my Bible to Acts 8:4 and asked him to read it.

He read, "*'They that were scattered abroad went every where preaching the word.'* Oh, yes," he said, "but these were the apostles."

"Will you be kind enough to read the first verse of the chapter?"

He read, "*'They were all scattered abroad…, except the apostles'*" (Acts 8:1). He had nothing more to say. What could he say?

Men and women, every man here who believes himself to be a Christian and is not winning others to Christ is disobedient to Jesus Christ. It is serious business in war to be disobedient to your commanding officer, and it is serious business for a Christian to be disobedient to Jesus Christ. Jesus says, "*Ye are my friends, if ye do whatsoever I command you*" (John 15:14).

One evening, I was told that a minister's son was to be present in my congregation, and that, though he professed to be a Christian, he did not work much at it. I watched for him and selected the man in the audience who I thought was he. At the close of the service, I hurried to the door by which he would leave and shook hands with people as they passed through it. When he came, I took his hand and said, "Good evening! I am glad to see you. Are you a friend of Jesus?"

"Yes," he replied heartily, "I consider myself a friend of Jesus."

"Jesus says, *'Ye are my friends, if ye do whatsoever I command you'"* (John 15:14).

His eyes fell. "If those are the conditions, I guess I am not."

I put the same question to you: Are you a friend of Jesus? Are you doing whatsoever He commands you? Are you winning souls as He commands? If I should ask every friend of Jesus to arise, could you conscientiously get up?

It Is a Sharing in Christ's Business of Life

In the second place, soulwinning should be the business of life with every Christian because it was the business of life with Jesus Christ Himself. What is it to be a Christian? To be a Christian is to be a follower of Christ. What is it to be a follower of Christ? To be a follower of Christ is to have the same purpose in life that Jesus Christ had. What was Christ's purpose in life? He Himself defines it in Luke 19:10: *"The Son of man is come to seek and to save that which was lost."* The Lord Jesus Christ had just one purpose in coming down to this earth. He had just one purpose in leaving the glory of heaven for the shame of earth. There was just one thing He lived for, one thing He suffered for, one thing He died for, and that was to save the lost. Is that your purpose? Is that what you live for? Is that the one great ambition of your life? Is that the all-absorbing passion of your life? If it is not, what right have you to call yourself a Christian? If Christ had one purpose in life, and you have an entirely different purpose in life, what right do you have to call yourself a follower of Jesus Christ? Jesus Christ says in Matthew 4:19, *"Follow me, and I will make you fishers of men."* Are you following Christ? Are you fishing for men?

Suppose, in a church service, I had asked every follower of Christ to stand up before preaching this message. I think that almost every man and woman in the audience would have stood. But suppose I should ask every follower of Christ to rise after sharing all of this; how many of them would stand up?

It Enables Us to Enjoy Personal Fellowship with Christ

In the third place, soulwinning should be the business of life with every Christian because it is the work in which we enjoy the unspeakable privilege of personal fellowship with Jesus Christ. There is a wonderful promise in the Bible, perhaps one of the most precious promises that it contains, and a promise that men and women are quoting constantly. I do not wonder that men and women so often quote the promise! What I do wonder is why they quote the promise without reference to the context and the condition. The promise is found in Matthew 28:20: *"Lo, I am with you always, even unto the end of the world."* Is there a more precious promise than that between the covers of this Book? Ah, but notice the condition. You will find it in the preceding verse, where Jesus says, *"Go ye therefore, and teach all nations,...and, lo, I am with you always, even unto the end of the world"* (Matthew 28:19–20). In other words, Jesus says, "You go My way, and I will go yours. You go out with Me in fellowship, in work, and I will go out with you in personal fellowship."

I want to ask you a question: Have you any right to this promise? You have often quoted it, you have often built upon it, but have you any right to it? Are you going out, as far as your line extends, and making disciples, winning souls? Your line may not extend very far, but, as far as your line extends, are you going out to bring other men or women to Christ? If you are, you have a right to that promise. If you are not, you have no right to that promise.

It Enables Us to Enjoy the Fullness of the Spirit's Presence and Power

In the fourth place, soulwinning should be the business of life with every one of us because it is the work in which we enjoy the fullness of the Holy Spirit's presence and power. Men and women, there is no greater blessing than to receive the Holy Spirit, to be filled with the Holy Spirit, to be baptized with the Holy Spirit. Oh, the joy of personally receiving and being filled with and baptized with the Holy Spirit! It is heaven come down to earth. But listen, that blessing is given for a specific purpose and can be had only along the line of its purpose. That purpose is revealed in Acts 1:8, where Jesus says, *"Ye shall receive power, after that the Holy Ghost is come upon you: and ye shall be witnesses unto me both in Jerusalem, and in all Judea, and in Samaria, and unto the uttermost parts of the earth."*

The baptism with the Holy Spirit, the gift of the Holy Spirit, is given to you and me to make us effective in God's service. There is many a man who is praying for the baptism with the Holy Spirit day after day, week after week, month after month, year after year, and getting nothing. Why? Because he is seeking a blessing that terminates in himself. He is seeking God's blessing but not seeking it on God's terms. When you are ready to go out and tell others about Christ as best you can, in God's power—when you are willing to go out and plead with men and women and children to accept the Lord Jesus Christ—then and only then can you have the gift of the Holy Spirit.

It Engages Us in Work That Produces the Most Beneficent Results

In the fifth place, soulwinning should be the business of life with every one of us because it is the work that produces the most beneficent results. There is no other work so beneficent, no other work that is for a moment comparable to the work of bringing other men and women to a saving knowledge of Jesus Christ. To feed the hungry, to clothe the naked, to house the poor, to instruct the ignorant, is blessed work, and I rejoice in all the work of that kind that is being done. But, men and women, to clothe the naked, to feed the hungry, to house the poor, to instruct the ignorant, is not for a moment to be compared with the glory, the honor, and the beneficence of bringing lost men and women to a saving knowledge of Jesus Christ. There is no work like it.

There is one passage in this Book that, if I could quote it as it ought to be quoted—that is, if I could so repeat the passage as to bring out the full meaning and force of three words in it—I would be willing to leave Birmingham without preaching another sermon; for if I could quote that passage as it ought to be quoted, if I could so quote it as to make you men and women realize the full and entire meaning and force of three words in that passage, everyone would rise en masse and go up and down the streets for days and weeks and months and years to come, beseeching men and women to be reconciled to God. You ask, "What is this passage?" It is a very familiar one. You all know it, but the trouble is that you know the words so well, you have never stopped to weigh the meaning. James 5:20 reads, *"Let him know, that he which converteth a sinner from the error of his way shall save a soul from death."* Oh, I would to God that I could burn these words into your hearts today: *"He which converteth a sinner from the error of his way shall save a soul from death."* The three words to note and weigh are *"save," "soul,"* and *"death."*

"Soul"

Let us begin with the middle of these three words, *"soul."* *"Shall save a soul from death."* Oh, if I only had power to make you men and women see the value of a soul, as God sees it—not merely the value of the soul of the philosopher, of the highly educated man, of the prince or the nobleman, but the value of the soul of the drunkard and the outcast woman; of the uneducated man and the ignoramus; of the ragged, dirty little boy or girl upon the street. Oh, if I could make you see and feel the value of one soul as God sees it!

What can I compare it with? Gold is nothing in comparison with the value of a soul. Precious stones are nothing; all the gems of earth are nothing. In 1893, during the World's Fair in Chicago, there was a place in the Manufactures and Liberal Arts Building, in the Tiffany exhibit, that I could never get close enough to see what the people were looking at. Time and time again, day after day, at all hours of the day and night, I went to that place; but there was always such a crowd there that, if I wanted to see what they were looking at, I had to stand on my tiptoes and look over the heads of the crowd in front of me. What were they looking at? Nothing but a cone of purple velvet revolving upon its axis, and toward its apex was a large, beautiful diamond of fabulous value. Day after day, people by the thousands came to see it; during the course of the World's Fair, people literally came by the million to look at that one stone. Well, it was worth looking at, but I have never thought of that sight since; yet the thought has occurred to me that the soul of one man or woman, the soul of the most worthless drunkard on the street, the soul of the vilest and most abandoned woman, the soul of the most ragged and filthiest and most ignorant boy or girl upon the street, is of infinitely more value in God's sight than ten thousand diamonds like that.

I had two friends in New York City in the same business, and both of them prospered in it. One of these men started in life in New York City practically penniless, but he had very rare business ability, and he succeeded in amassing a fortune of first a million dollars, then of two million dollars, then of three million dollars, and then of four million dollars. One day, he was walking toward his beautiful home up on Fifth Avenue, and as he crossed one of the lower avenues of the city, he was run into by a tramcar and taken home to die. He left four million dollars. Yes, he left it all. He did not take a penny of it with him. And I remember how the New York and the Brooklyn papers came out with editorials upon this self-made man, speaking of his remarkable business ability. He had come to New York as a young man absolutely without money and had gone to work and amassed a fortune of four million dollars. Then he died.

The other man was in the same business. He, too, had prospered. I don't know just how much he had accumulated; I think it was about a half million dollars. Then, one day, God came into that man's home and took out of it a beautiful daughter, a child only four years of age, the idol of that man's heart. A few days after her burial, he was riding up in the elevated train toward his home, and as he thought of his little daughter, his eyes were blinded with tears, so he held the newspaper up before his face to hide the tears from the strangers in the train. He kept thinking about his little daughter Florence, and this question came into his heart: *Your daughter is dead; what are you doing for other men's daughters?* He thought, *I am doing nothing, but I will.* The next year, he put ten thousand dollars into the rescue of fallen girls in New York City; the following year, he put eleven thousand dollars into the same work; and the year after that, he put himself into the work. He turned his back upon his place of business down on Fulton Street, and I have oftentimes known of his not going to his place of business more than two hours a week, and spending eighteen or twenty hours a day down in the slums of New York City, seeking those who were perishing. Finally, he turned his back on the business altogether, capitalized it, and gave his whole time and strength to going up and down the streets, telling lost men and women about Jesus Christ. He is upward of seventy years of age—the youngest seventy-year-old man I know. God has used him to lift thousands of men and women from the deepest depths of sin to a saving knowledge of Jesus Christ.

Now I am going to ask you a question. In the light of eternity, in the light of that great judgment day to which we are all hurrying, which of these two men made the better use of his time, talents, and money—the man who devoted his entire energies to saving four million dollars and then left it all and died, entering eternity a pauper, or the man who devoted his strength to saving thousands of souls, who will meet and welcome him in a glorious eternity?

"Death"

The second word—*"death." "Shall save a soul from death."* Oh, men and women, the word *death* is one of the most awful words in our language. People in our day, poets and theologians, try to paint death in fair colors. There is nothing fair about death. Death is a hideous thing; death is a horrid thing; death is an appalling thing; death is our enemy. Thank God that, for the Christian, it is a conquered enemy; for Jesus Christ has abolished death and brought life and immortality to light through the gospel. But death itself is an appalling thing.

Now, listen: When you go to a man, woman, or child and lead him or her to a saving knowledge of Jesus Christ, you have saved a soul from death. Remember, the death of the soul does not mean mere nonexistence; death does not mean annihilation; death does not mean mere cessation of being; death does not mean mere nonexistence any more than life in the New Testament means mere existence. Life means right existence, holy existence, Godlike existence, the ennoblement and the glorification and the deification of existence; and death means just the opposite. Death means wrong existence; unholy existence; the corruption and the defilement and the debasement and the shame and the ignominy and the ruin and the despair of existence. When you and I lead a man or woman to Christ, we save a soul from death.

"Save"

Then, look at that other word—*"save." "Shall save a soul from death."* That is one of the great words. Oh, you sometimes narrow it down and make it a very small sort of word, but, as it is used in the Bible, the word *save* is a magnificent word. It means not merely to save from but to save *to*; not merely to save from hell but to save to glory, to save to holiness, to save to happiness, to save to heaven, to save to a knowledge of God, to save to communion with God, to save to likeness to God.

Suppose I were to tell all the businessmen about a process whereby they could go out through the streets and country roads, stoop down in the mud and dirt, pick up ordinary stones, and, by the mysterious process of the lapidary, which I would tell them of, transform them into real diamonds of the very first quality. Suppose such a process really existed. Do you think there would be anybody who wouldn't want to know about it? There would be more people than imaginable coming to find out how to do it. Men and women, I can tell you that very thing. I can tell you how to go out through the streets, out into your country roads; stoop down in the mud and dirt and mire of sin; pick out the common, ordinary, rude stones of lost souls; and, by the glorious art of the soulwinner, transform them into diamonds worthy of a place in the Savior's eternal diadem. Don't you think that is worthwhile? Is anything else so well worthwhile?

It Brings the Most Abundant Reward

Once more, soulwinning should be the business of life with every Christian because it is the work that brings the most abundant reward. There is another verse I wish might sink into your heart. It is Daniel 12:3: *"They that be wise shall shine as the brightness of the firmament; and they that turn many to righteousness as the stars for ever and ever."* Some people want to shine down here. Men and women, it is not worthwhile. The brightest star in any earthly galaxy will soon fade. The brightest star in the financial firmament, the brightest star in the political firmament, the brightest star in the social firmament—how long will they shine? Only a few years, and then they will go out forever.

The brightest star in our political firmament about three years ago (at this time, a star that shone with absolutely unrivaled splendor, a man about whom the world was speaking and whose name the world was beginning to couple with the names of America's greatest statesmen, such as Washington and Lincoln)—one dark night, that star was snuffed out by the crack of the revolver of a half-crazy anarchist; and today, that great statesman is practically forgotten. In America, almost no one ever speaks about McKinley today. You can look through our papers, day after day, and never see his name. It is all Roosevelt now; it used to be all McKinley. Ten years from now, it will all be somebody else. It is so here in England. You go through your English papers today, and it is all Chamberlain now. Ten years from now, Chamberlain will be practically forgotten.

It doesn't pay to shine down here. It does pay to shine up there. They that shine up there shall shine as the stars forever and ever. (See Daniel 12:3.) Men and women, most of us could not shine down here if we wanted to; but, thank God, there is not one of us who can't shine up there. There is only one way to shine up there, and that is by saving the lost, by bringing them to a saving knowledge of Christ.

Before I close, I must tell you a story. This incident is so remarkable that when I first heard it, it seemed to me that it could not possibly be true. Yet the man who told it was of such a character that I felt that it must be true because he told it, and yet I said, "I must find out for myself whether that story is true or not." So, I went to the librarian of the university where the incident was said to have occurred, and I found out that it was true. The story, as I tell it to you today, is as I got it from the brother of the main actor in the scene.

The story is this: About twelve miles from where I live, twelve miles from the city of Chicago, is the suburb of Evanston, where there is a large Methodist university, I think the largest university of the Methodist denomination in America; in all events, a very great university. Years ago, before the college had blossomed into a great university, there were many students in it, and among them were two young country boys from the state of Iowa—strong, vigorous fellows, one of them a famous swimmer. Early one morning, word came to the college that down on Lake Michigan, just off the shores of Evanston, there was a wreck. It proved to be the *Lady Elgin*. The college boys, with everybody else in town, hurried down to the shores of Lake Michigan. Off yonder in the distance, they saw the *Lady Elgin* going to pieces.

Edward Spencer, the famous swimmer, threw off all his superfluous garments, tied a rope round his waist, threw one end to his comrades on the shore, sprang into Lake Michigan, swam out to the wreck, grasped someone who was drowning, and gave the sign to be pulled ashore. And again and again and again, he swam out, grasped a drowning man or woman, and brought him or her safe to shore, until he had brought to shore a seventh, an eighth, a ninth, and a tenth. Then he was utterly exhausted.

Those who were there had built a fire of logs upon the sand. He went and stood by the fire of logs on that cold, bleak morning, blue, pinched, trembling, hardly able to stand. He stood before that fire, trying to get a little warmth into his perishing members. As he stood there, he turned and looked round on Lake Michigan, and off in the distance, near the *Lady Elgin*, he saw men and women still struggling in the water. He said, "Boys, I am going in again."

"No, no, Ed," they cried. "It is utterly vain to try. You have used up all your strength; you could not save anybody. For you to jump into the lake will simply mean for you to commit suicide."

"Well, boys," he said, "they are drowning, and I will try, anyhow." And he started to the shore of the lake.

His companions cried, "No, no, Ed—no, don't try."

He said, "I will." Then he jumped into Lake Michigan and battled out against the waves and got hold of a drowning man who was struggling in the water. And he did so again and again and again, until he had brought an eleventh, a twelfth, a thirteenth, a fourteenth, and a fifteenth safely to shore.

Then they pulled him in through the breakers. He could scarcely get to the fire on the beach, and there, trembling, he stood before that fire, trying to get a little warmth into his shivering limbs. As they looked at him, it seemed as if the hand of death was already upon him. Then he turned away from the fire again and looked over the lake, and as he looked away off yonder in the distance, he saw a spar rising and falling upon the waves. He looked at it with his keen eye and saw a man's head above the spar. He said, "Boys, there's a man trying to save himself." He looked again and saw a woman's head beside the man's. He said, "Boys, there's a man trying to save his wife." He watched the spar as it drifted toward the point. He knew that to drift around that point meant certain death. He said, "Boys, I am going to help him."

"No, no, Ed," they cried. "You can't help him. Your strength is all gone."

He responded, "I will try, anyway." He sprang into Lake Michigan, swam out wearily toward the spar, and, reaching it, put his hands upon the spar, summoned all his dying strength, and brought that spar around the right end of the point to safety. Then they pulled him in through the breakers, and loving hands lifted him from the beach and carried him to his room up in the college. They laid him upon his bed, made a fire in the grate, and his brother Will remained by to watch him, for he was becoming delirious. As the day passed on, Will Spencer sat by the fire. Suddenly, he heard a gentle footfall behind him and felt someone touch him on the back. He looked up, and there stood Ed, looking wistfully down into his face. He said, "What is it, Ed?"

He replied, "Will, did I do my best?"

"Why, Ed," he said, "you saved seventeen."

He said, "I know that, but I was afraid I didn't do my very best. Will, do you think I did my very best?"

Will took him back to bed and laid him upon it and sat down by his side. As the night passed, I am told, Ed went into semi-delirium, and Will sat by the bed and held his hand and tried to calm him. All that he thought about were the men and women who perished that day; for, even with all his bravery, many went down to a watery grave. Will sat there and held Ed's hand and tried to calm him. "Ed," he said, "you saved seventeen."

He said, "I know it, Will, I know it; but, oh, if only I could have saved just one more."

Men and women, you and I stand this afternoon beside a stormy sea. Oh, as we look out at this tossing sea of life round about us on every hand, there are wrecks. Will you and I sit here calmly while the passengers are going down, going down, going down, going down to a hopeless eternity?

Men and women, let us plunge in again and again and again and again, until every last ounce of strength is gone; and when at last, in sheer exhaustion, we fall upon the shore in the earnestness of our love for perishing men, let us cry, "Oh, if only I could save just one more."

THE MOST EFFECTIVE METHOD OF SOULWINNING

"[Andrew] first findeth his own brother Simon…. And he brought him to Jesus."
—John 1:41–42

Andrew brought his brother to Jesus. We are not told that he ever preached a sermon in his life. If he did, the Holy Spirit did not think it was worth recording; but this brother whom he brought to Jesus preached a sermon that led three thousand people to Jesus in one day. Where would Simon Peter's sermon have been if it had not been for Andrew's personal work? The most important kind of Christian work in the world is personal work. We look at the men who stand on the platform and speak to great crowds; but I believe God pays more attention to the man who sits down with a single soul.

A blind woman once came to my office in Chicago and asked, "You don't think my blindness will keep me from doing Christian work, do you?"

"No," I replied. "On the contrary, I think it might be a great help to you. A great many people, seeing your blindness, will come and sit down with you, and you can talk with them about the Savior."

"That is not what I mean. I don't want to talk to one person. When a woman can talk to five hundred or six hundred, she don't want to spend time talking to one."

"Your Master could talk to five thousand at once, for we have it on record, and He did not think it beneath His dignity to talk to one at a time."

Have you ever thought of the tremendous power that there is in personal, hand-to-hand work?

One day, a man in Boston had in his Sunday school class a boy fresh from the country. He was a very dull boy, and he knew almost nothing about the Bible. He did not even know where to look to find the gospel of John. He was very much put out because the other boys were bright boys and knew their Bibles. He was just a green country boy, seventeen years of age; but that Sunday school teacher had a heart full of love for Christ and for perishing souls. So, one day, he went down into the boot shop where that boy worked and asked him, "Would you not like to be a Christian?" The boy had never been approached that way before. Nobody had ever spoken to him about his soul.

He said, "Yes, I would like to be a Christian." And that Sunday school teacher explained what it meant to be a Christian and then said, "Let us pray."

They knelt down in the back of that boot shop, and the boy, as far as he knew, became a Christian. That boy was Dwight L. Moody. If it had not been for Edward Kimball's faithful, personal work, where would Dwight L. Moody and his great work throughout the world have been?

Probably there are some Sunday school teachers here who say, "I wish I could get down to the great meeting in the big hall; but I have to stay here teaching a lot of little boys or girls." Who knows who there is in that little class of yours? Who knows what your ignorant, ragged little boy may become? Every teacher, make up your mind, by God's help, that you will at least make an honest effort to lead everybody in your Sunday school class to Christ today. This world will never be saved by preaching; but this world could soon be evangelized by personal work.

Let us see. Let us suppose there are two thousand people reading this at some point. Suppose every one of you became a personal worker, and suppose, by your very best effort, you succeeded in leading only one to Christ in a year. Then that one led another person to Christ the next year, and so on. What would be the result? At the end of the year, there would be 4,000; at the end of two years, there would be 8,000; at the end of three years, 16,000; at the end of four years, 32,000; at the end of five years, 64,000; at the end of six years, 128,000; at the end of seven years, 256,000; and at the end of eight years, your whole city would be won for Christ. At the end of thirty-five years, every man, woman, and child on the face of the earth would have heard the gospel. There is not one who cannot lead at least one to Christ this year. You can instruct everyone whom you lead to Christ to go out and be a soulwinner. After you get hold of someone, and he is saved, send him out to lead others, and, each of them bringing one, and that one bringing in another, you will soon touch the whole city.

Now let us talk about the advantages of personal evangelism.

Anybody Can Do It

The first advantage of personal evangelism is that anybody can do it. You cannot all preach; I am glad you can't. What an institution this world would be if we were all preachers! You cannot all sing; I am glad you can't, for if you could, then a great singer would be no curiosity, and you would not come out to hear him sing. You can't all even teach Sunday school classes. Some people have an idea that any converted person can teach a Sunday school class. I don't believe it. I think we are making a great mistake in this respect, in setting unqualified persons to teach in Sunday schools; but there is not a child of God who cannot do personal work. A mother with a large family knows she is not called to be a preacher (at least, I hope she does), but she can do personal work better than anybody else.

A lady came to me one time—she had five children—and said (I think she had been reading *The Life of Frances E. Willard*), "I wish I could do some work like that for Christ."

I said, "You can work for Christ among all the people you move among." I watched that woman. Every one of her children was brought to Christ—every one! Every maid who came to work in that home was dealt with about her soul. Every butcher's boy or grocer's boy who came around to the door was dealt with about his soul. Every time she went out shopping, she made it a point to talk with the man or woman behind the counter. And when, one dark day, death came into that home and took away a sweet little child, she did not forget to speak to the undertaker, who came to do the last offices for the dead, about his soul. He told me that no one had ever impressed him as that woman had, in the midst of her sorrow, being interested in his soul.

An invalid can do personal work. I have a friend in New York City who left a life of wealth and fashion to go out to work among the outcast. One day, she got hold of a poor outcast girl. She did not live much more than a year after that lady had led her to Christ. She took her to her home to die. As Delia was dying, she wrote to her friends, some in Sing Sing Prison, some in the Tombs of New York City—all her friends were among the criminal class—about Christ. Those who were not behind prison bars she invited to come and see her.

My friend told me, "There was a constant procession up the stairway of outcast women and men who came to see Delia, and I knew, before Delia died, of one hundred of the most hopeless men and women in New York City whom she had led to Christ."

That puts us to shame! Suppose that God kindled a fire in your heart, that you received the anointing of the Spirit of Christ, and that every one of you started out to do personal work. You would not need any evangelist to come from abroad. That is what we have come for—to stir you up to do it.

You Can Do It Anywhere

The second advantage about personal evangelism is that you can do it anywhere. You cannot preach in every place. You can preach in the churches two or three times a week; you can preach in the town hall occasionally; you can preach in the streets sometimes. But you cannot go down in the factories and preach often; you cannot go there and hold services. Yet you can go there and do personal work, if you just hire out there.

One man who came to our meetings in Liverpool from Hudson's dry soap factory was converted, and every once in a while, I would get a letter telling me of their meetings there. Now they even have a meeting that they conduct outside the building somewhere. In Bradley's foundry, a workman got an invitation to the meetings, but he could not go, so he handed it over to the wickedest man in the shop. The man was grateful for the invitation, thought the workman would appreciate it if he went, and was saved at the very first meeting. He went back and told his companions, and there was a revival in the foundry.

A telegraph messenger boy was converted in Manchester, and before we were through, there were seventy messenger boys saved in Manchester. There is not a hotel or a factory or a public house where you cannot do work.

You Can Do It at Any Time

The third advantage to personal evangelism is that you can do it at any time—any hour of the night, 365 days a year (366 in a leap year). Certainly, you cannot preach every hour of the day. If you preach three times a day, you are doing well; but there is not an hour of the day or night, between twelve one night and twelve the next, that you cannot do personal work. You can go out on the streets at night and find the poor wanderers.

When I lived in Minneapolis, I employed a missionary to go out on the streets at night to speak to the drunkards, outcast women, and night workers; and some of the best conversions were among these people. She had been an outcast herself at one time and was leading them to the Christ whom she had found.

Soon after Mr. Moody was converted, he made up his mind that he would not let a day go by without speaking to someone about his soul. One night, he came home late—it was nearly ten o'clock. He said, "Here, I haven't spoken to my man today. I guess I have lost my chance." Then he saw a man standing under the lamp-light, and he said to himself, *There's my last chance.* He hurried up to him and asked, "Are you a Christian?"

"It's none of your business, and if you were not a sort of preacher, I would knock you into the gutter."

"Well," Mr. Moody said, "I just wanted to lead you to Christ."

The next day, that man went to a friend of Mr. Moody's and said, "That man Moody has got zeal without knowledge. He spoke to me in the street last night and asked me if I was a Christian. It is none of his business. If he had not been a sort of preacher, I would have knocked him down. He has got zeal without knowledge. He is doing more harm than good."

Mr. Moody's friend went to him and said, "See here, Moody, it is all right to be in earnest; but you have got zeal without knowledge. You are doing more harm than good." (Let me say here that it is better to have zeal without knowledge than knowledge without zeal.)

So Mr. Moody went out, feeling rather cheap and crestfallen. A few weeks passed, and one night, there was an awful pounding at his door. Mr. Moody got up and opened the door, and there was this very man. He said, "Mr. Moody, I have not had a night's peace since you spoke to me that night under the lamppost. I have come to ask you to show me how to be a Christian." Mr. Moody took him in and showed him the way of life; and when the Civil War broke out, that man went and laid down his life for his country.

Another time, the thought came to Mr. Moody after he was in bed, *You have not spoken to your man today*. But he said, "I am in bed. I cannot get up and go out now." Yet he could not rest, so he got up and went and opened the door, and it was pouring rain. "Well," he said, "there is no use going out on the street this awful night. There won't be a soul out in this pouring rain." Just then, he heard the patter of a man's feet and saw him coming. As he came up, Mr. Moody rushed out and said, "Can I have the shelter of your umbrella?"

"Certainly."

"Have you got a shelter in the time of storm?" he asked, and he pointed him to Jesus.

It Reaches All Classes

The fourth advantage of personal evangelism is that it reaches all classes. There are a great many people who cannot be reached in any other way than by personal work. Thousands of people could not come to church if they would, and thousands would not come to church if they could. There are splendid halls, just adapted for our purpose, that will hold about 10,000 women and 10,000 men—20,000 people inside—and there will be 580,000 outside. It is the 580,000 that we are after. You cannot reach them by the church, you cannot reach them by open-air meetings, you cannot reach them by rescue missions. There is only one way you can reach them, and that is by personal work. There is not a man, woman, or child whom you cannot reach by personal work. You can reach the policemen, the tramcar men, and the railway men. There is not anybody you cannot reach by personal work.

It Hits the Mark

The fifth advantage to personal evangelism is that it hits the mark. In preaching, you have to be more or less general. In personal work, you have just one man, just one woman, to talk to, and you can hit the mark every time.

Perhaps you have heard of Henry Ward Beecher. He went out shooting with his father one day. He had often gone before, but he had never shot anything in his life. Way down yonder was a squirrel. His father said, "Henry, do you see that squirrel?"

"Yes, Father."

"Would you like to hit it?"

"Yes, Father; but I never hit anything in my life."

"Lay the barrel of your gun across the top rail down here," he said, "and look right down along the barrel. Henry, do you see the squirrel?"

"Yes, Father."

"Well, pull the trigger."

He pulled the trigger, and the squirrel fell at the first shot. It was the first thing he ever shot in his life. Why? Because it was the first thing he had ever aimed at.

That is the trouble with a good deal of our preaching—we aim at nothing and hit it every time. This is the advantage of personal work: We can aim at one definite person. But in our preaching, as Mr. Moody used to say, "I speak to this lady on the front seat, and she passes it over her shoulder to the man back of her, and he passes it to the woman back of him, and she passes it to the man back of her, and they keep passing it on till they pass it out the back door." We have a wonderful power of applying the good points of a sermon to somebody else. When it comes to personal work, there is nobody else to apply it to. I try to be personal in my preaching; but, be just as personal as you can, and yet you will miss your mark.

A man came to my church one morning, unctuous—not having unction, but unctuous—a man who was talking all the time about "the deeper life" but who had not had an ordinary, decent, everyday kind of Christian life. He had all the phraseology of the deepest Christian experience, he talked about being filled with the Spirit, but he cheated other people in business. I saw him coming into the audience, and I said to myself, *I am glad you have come. I will hit you this morning. I have a sermon just adapted to you.* While I was preaching, I planned to look right at him, so he would know I meant him; and he sat there, beaming up at me. And when the sermon was over, he came down to me, rubbing his hands. "Oh," he said, "Brother Torrey, I came eight miles to hear you this morning. I have enjoyed it."

That was just what I did not want. I wanted to make him miserable. But now I had Jim face-to-face, and he did not enjoy what

I had to say. That is the advantage of personal work. You can aim right square at the mark and still hit it. A man can stand to hear preaching all day, but he will say, "I don't like this personal work." It hits too hard. You don't like to have a person come up and ask, "Are you a Christian?" The minister can preach all he pleases, but when he looks you right in the eye, you know he is talking to you. He aims right straight at the mark and hits it.

It Is Effective

The sixth advantage to personal evangelism is that it is effective. Personal work succeeds where every other kind of work fails. I don't care who the preacher is or how good a preacher he may be; a man or a woman who has not been affected by the sermon will be reached by some very ordinary person with the love of God and of souls. Take Mr. Moody, for example. I think Mr. Moody was as good a preacher as I have ever heard. I would rather listen to Mr. Moody preach a sermon that I have heard a dozen times than to listen to any other man preach a sermon I have never heard at all; but, as good a preacher as Mr. Moody was, thousands of people would go out utterly unmoved by his sermons. I have seen very ordinary working people, uneducated people, but people who had the love of Christ and of souls in their heart, get hold of the man or woman who had gone out of Mr. Moody's meeting utterly untouched and, in ten or fifteen minutes, lead him or her to the Lord Jesus Christ.

It Meets Every Need of the Individual

The seventh advantage of personal evangelism is that it meets the specific need, and every need, of the individual. Even when a man comes to Christ, he has difficulties and doubts, troubles and questions. He cannot ask them of the preacher. How often a man sits down in the audience and says, "I wish I could speak to that preacher alone." In this personal, hand-to-hand work, a man can ask all the questions he wants to, and you can meet all his difficulties.

I am getting letters from people all over the world who have difficulties. My father used to tell a story (he did not vouch for its truth) of a physician in the village who had a jug. He took a little of every kind of medicine he had in his shop, put it in that jug, and shook it up; and when anyone came to him with something the matter, and he did not know just what that matter was, he would give him or her a spoonful out of that jug, thinking that there was something in it that would meet the case, anyhow.

That is what we do in our preaching—we take a little comfort and put it in the sermon, a little bit of conviction, a little bit to show the way of life, and then we shake it all up and give it to the people. If I were going to be doctored, I would want the doctor to find out my specific difficulty, and I would want to take the kind of medicine that met my specific need. In personal work, you give specific passages of Scripture for specific difficulties.

It Produces Abundant Results

The eighth advantage of personal evangelism is that it produces abundant results. The great services, where the ministers speak to five hundred or a thousand or five thousand people, do not produce as abundant results. Suppose a man were pastor of a church of a hundred members, and suppose he was a very faithful minister and that, as a result of his preaching, there were added to his church each year fifty people on confession of faith. That would be a pretty good record. In the report of the Presbyterian churches of America, there were only two hundred of the seven thousand that reported over fifty accessions for the year. But suppose, by his faithful preaching, this pastor added fifty a year. Now, suppose that pastor said, "I am going to train my people to do personal work," and he indeed trained his people to do personal work; but suppose only one half of them would consent to do it. Suppose that each of these fifty trained workers succeeded in winning only one a month to Christ. That would mean six hundred a year. Preaching is not in it with personal work.

But, friends, some of us think we pay the minister to do the work. You don't do anything of the kind. Your minister is your leader, and you are supposed to work under his leadership. One reason why the church of which I am pastor always has a revival is because the people are trained to do personal work. We have had a revival ever since I have been pastor of it, which has been for ten years. There have been ten years of revival. There has never been a month that we have not received new members. There has never been a Sabbath without conversions. We would not know what to make of it if there were a Sabbath without conversions. I do not think there has been any day in the week of all this time—3,650 in all—that someone has not been won to Christ in or about the building. There will be a good many people converted this Sabbath. You ask, "Who is going to preach?" I don't know. But whoever preaches, there will be conversions; and in the Sabbath school, there will be conversions; and there will be conversions in the evening meeting, as well. Why? Because I have a church that believes in and does personal work. Every Sunday evening while I preach, I know there is someone right near every person in that church who knows how to lead a soul to Christ. There are workers in every section of the church. If anybody gets up and goes out, I know that there is at least one person who is going to be spoken to that night. Someone will drop down the stairs behind him, perhaps follow him a block or two, before he speaks to him.

Go out to the people and ask God to give you power. The Holy Spirit is for every one of us. I do thank God that the great gift of the Son is for the whole world, and that the gift of the Holy Spirit is for every saved one. *"If ye then, being evil, know how to give good gifts unto your children, how much more shall your Father which is in heaven give good things to them that ask him?"* (Matthew 7:11). Just ask, and then go out. Of course, you need to know something about your Bibles in order to do personal work, but you need only one text to start with.

When Mr. Moody first came to New Haven, we thought we would go out and hear this strange, uneducated man. I was in the senior class in the theological department of the university and was just about to take my BD degree. I knew more then than I will ever know in my life again. We thought we would patronize Mr. Moody a little bit. He did not seem at all honored by our presence, but, as we heard him speak, we learned that though he was uneducated, he knew some things we didn't. Some of us had sense enough to go to him and say, "Mr. Moody, we wish you would tell us how to do it."

He told us to come round early the next night, and he would tell us. We theologians went up to the meeting, and he said a few words to us, gave us a few texts of Scripture, and then said, "You go at it." The best way to learn how to do it is to do it. *"He that goeth forth and weepeth, bearing precious seed, shall doubtless come again with rejoicing, bringing his sheaves with him"* (Psalm 126:6). If, however, you make a stupid blunder the first time, go at it again. But if you never start until you are sure you will not make a blunder, you will make the biggest blunder of your life. Go alone with God first, and see if you are right with Him; put away every known sin out of your life, surrender absolutely to God, ask for the Holy Spirit, and then pitch in.

17

SIMPLE METHODS BY WHICH ANYONE CAN WIN OTHERS TO CHRIST

*"Then the Spirit said unto Philip, Go near,
and join thyself to this chariot. And Philip ran thither to
him, and heard him read the prophet Esaias, and said,
Understandest thou what thou readest?"*
—Acts 8:29–30

One of the greatest joys on earth is the joy of bringing others to a saving knowledge of Christ. I have heard people say that when they were converted, the whole world seemed different; the sun seemed to shine with a new light, there was new music in the song of the birds, all nature seemed clothed with new beauty and glory. I had no such experience when I was saved. In fact, I was saved in the middle of the night, and the sun was not shining at all. But I did have such an experience the first time that I led another person to a definite acceptance of Jesus Christ as his definite Savior.

I had been dealing with this person for two solid hours and seemed to be making but little headway. Then, at the very close, he yielded and accepted Christ. When I left the building where this decision had been made, it was nearly sunset in the springtime, and the whole world seemed to have a beauty that I had never seen in it before. It seemed as if I were walking on air; my heart was filled with joy such as I had never known before. There is no other joy like the joy of saving men, and it is possible for every child of God, no matter how humble and ungifted, to have this joy.

God's most approved method of winning others to Christ is indicated in Acts 8:29–30—the method of personal, hand-to-hand dealing with the lost. The high estimate that God places upon this form of work is seen in the context of this Scripture. Philip was in the midst of a great revival in Samaria, with great crowds assembling daily to listen, when an apparently strange command came to arise and leave this great work that had stirred the whole city, and to go down into the way that leads from Jerusalem into Gaza, *"which is desert"* (Acts 8:26). Wise as he was, and strange as the order must have seemed, Philip, without a moment's questioning or hesitation, *"arose and went"* (Acts 8:27). An inquiring soul passed by in his chariot, and the Spirit of God whispered to Philip, *"Go near, and join thyself to this chariot. And Philip ran"* (Acts 8:29–30).

Would that we were as prompt to obey the first whisper of the Spirit when He bids us go and speak to others. Our Master did not consider it beneath Him to speak to one at a time. We have more frequent records of His dealing with individuals than we have of His preaching sermons to vast audiences. The one-by-one method of soulwinning is the method that God delights to honor. But how shall we do it?

Select a Man to Win

In personal work, as in all forms of work, definiteness is of tremendous importance. There are hosts of people who have a longing to win someone to Christ, but they do not pick out any definite individual to win, and so they fail. A definite purpose to lead some definite individual to a definite acceptance of a definite Savior will accomplish vastly more than an indefinite longing to lead an indefinite number of indefinite persons with some definite experiences. But how shall we select the individuals whom we are to win to Christ?

Pray

There are some who are the peculiar property of each of us. We can lead them to Christ, and no one else can. Who these persons are, God alone knows; but He is willing to tell us, if we will only ask Him. We should go to Him and ask Him to show us who the persons are whom He would have us to lead to Christ. Then we should wait upon Him, listening for His voice—it is a still, small voice (see 1 Kings 19:12)—as it speaks in our hearts. When He mentions a person, we should write down his or her name and determine that we will lead him or her to Christ.

Select Those Who Are Accessible

The most accessible of all people are those in our own family, and that is the place to begin—in your own home. Jesus said to the demoniac whom He had healed, and who wished to accompany Him on His missionary journeys, *"Return to thine own house, and show how great things God hath done unto thee"* (Luke

8:39). When Andrew found Christ, he went first of all to his own brother Simon and *"brought him to Jesus"* (John 1:42). None of us should rest as long as any member of our own household is unsaved. I do not mean that we should confine our efforts to them but that we should begin with them and keep after them.

There are those who say that the hardest persons to lead to Christ are those in our own households. This is not true. If your life is right with God, no one will know it as well as those who live with you, and no one else can influence them as well as you can. The holiest and sweetest privilege that a father or mother has is the privilege of bringing his or her own children to Christ. This we are commanded by the Word of God to do in Ephesians 6:4: *"And, ye fathers, provoke not your children to wrath: but bring them up in the nurture and admonition of the Lord."* And this we can do, for God does not command the impossible.

I should feel that my wife and I had been robbed of one of the sweetest privileges of life if anyone other than us should lead one of our children to Christ. Of course, I would infinitely rather they would be led by someone else to Christ than not to be led at all, but it is our sacred privilege to do it ourselves.

Next to those in your own family are those with whom you are associated in business or in work. If you are a shop assistant, go to work with your own shop mates; if you are a laboring man, go to work with your fellow laborers; if you are a businessman, go to work with your partners and your employees; if you are a student, go to work with your fellow students. Try first for the man next to you. I meet many people who wish to win men in China to Christ but who are not willing to make any strong effort to win the unsaved members in their own homes, or their next-door neighbors, to Christ. It is a suicidal policy to send anyone out as a foreign missionary who has not first demonstrated his love for souls and his capacity to win them to Christ by winning others to Christ at home.

Select Those Who Are Approachable

Same Age

Those of the same age are, as a rule, more approachable than those of a widely differing age. Young men are best to deal with young men, middle-aged men with middle-aged men, and old men with old men. Children often have more influence with children than adults do.

Same Sex

Select those of the same sex, as a rule. That rule has a few exceptions, but not many; it is best for men to deal with men, and women to deal with women. Immense mischief has come through the disregard of this rule of practical wisdom. I always take it as a bad sign when I see young men who are constantly dealing with young women, or young women who are constantly dealing with young men. I have never known a case of this kind that has not turned out badly. Some of the saddest tragedies I have ever known have come through mistakes of this sort. Of course, an elderly, motherly woman can deal wisely with young men and boys, and, occasionally, elderly men can deal wisely with little girls and young women; but a long experience with Christian workers has strengthened in me the conviction of the wisdom of this rule— men with men and women with women.

Same Station in Life

Select people of the same station in life. This rule also has exceptions. There are notable instances on record where servants have led their masters to Christ (the great Earl of Shaftesbury was led to Christ by a nurse in the home); but, as a rule, people can be most readily approached by others in the same class of society. No one can deal as well with a lawyer as another lawyer; no one can deal as well with a physician as another physician; no one, as a rule, can deal as well with an artisan as a fellow artisan; no one can deal as effectively with a student as a fellow student.

Congenial Disposition

Select those who are congenial. To all of us, some people are congenial, and others are not. Just why they are congenial, we cannot always tell; but we know it is a fact. There are those who take to my friend Alexander who do not take to me, and there are those who take to me who do not take to Alexander. Now, those who take to me are the ones for me to deal with, and those who take to Alexander are the people for Alexander to deal with. Alexander can reach people whom I could not touch, but I can reach people whom Alexander cannot touch. However, we may account for these things—they are facts, and a wise soul-winner will always take account of facts. He concerns himself more with facts than with the philosophy of the facts; he acts upon the facts and lets the philosophy of them take care of itself. There is not a person who has not some acquaintance whom he alone can touch.

You are responsible before God for that one person. You need not confine yourself absolutely to those whom you select to win—be always ready at the slightest opening of opportunity to win anyone to Christ who comes your way. But make a specialty of the one you do select. Never lose sight of the fact that you are to win that person for Christ, and never rest until he or she is won.

Lay Siege to Him

When you have selected your person to win, the next thing is to lay siege to him. Do you know what it is to lay siege to a soul? Have you ever selected a certain individual and laid siege to him to win him to Christ, cost what it might, take as long as it might?

You know how an insurance agent conducts his business. He goes into a town and selects those who seem to him to be likely risks, and then he lays siege to them. He writes them letters, sends them literature, calls upon them, persistently follows up with them, and studies them. He learns their tastes and observes how they can best be approached, and he never rests until he has insured these persons whom he has selected to insure. I have had some experience with the persistent attentions of these insurance agents, and I have nothing to say against their pertinacity; I simply want to recommend their methods to soulwinners. Ought we not to be as businesslike and as much in earnest about insuring people for eternity as an insurance agent is about insuring people for a time? He does it for the money that he can make out of it; we do it for a higher object—the glory of God and the salvation of those whom we are pursuing. But how shall we lay siege to them?

Lay Siege through Prayer

When you have selected a person to win for Christ, you should pursue him or her by prayer day and night, day after day, week after week, and, if need be, year after year. In order to be definite, make a prayer list. Write on a sheet of paper, "God helping me, I promise to pray earnestly and work persistently for the salvation of the following persons," then kneel down and ask God to tell you whom to put on that list. Do not make it too long. When you have written it, keep your promise. One by one, as those whom you have prayed for accept Christ, you can take their names off the list and add others.

Everywhere we have gone around the world, we have had people make such prayer lists as this, and people are constantly

242 Real Salvation

coming to us and telling us, "Another one gone off my prayer list." One of the leading businessmen of Belfast, an active Christian worker, made such a prayer list when we were in that city. He came to me toward the close of the mission and said, "The last one has gone off my prayer list today. They have all been saved."

Lay Siege by Personal Effort

It is well to pray, but it is not enough to pray. Praying for the salvation of others is an act of insincerity unless we are willing to go to those for whom we pray, talk with them, and beseech them to be reconciled to God. Sometimes, you will not go at the conquest of the soul directly; you will first prepare the way.

Last season, while I was going round the country holding missions, my family resided in Southport. I would go there to spend my holidays. The first time I went there, I met a man whom God laid upon my heart, and whom I determined to win for Christ. He was a most unlikely case. He had once been in a good position but had gone down through drink. I began to cultivate his acquaintance, gained his friendship, and watched for my opportunity to win him for Christ. Every time I met him on the street, I would speak with him. When he became disposed to show me little acts of kindness, I accepted them in order to win him. Time after time, I met him, and the opportunity to speak about the great question did not come.

When I was speaking in Manchester, I referred to him and how I was waiting for an opportunity, and a man in the audience said to another, "Well, he will die before he speaks to him." But he was mistaken. I was watching and praying, God was listening, and the opportunity came.

I returned from a mission and heard that this man had caught cold and was quite ill. I met his daughter and asked if I could see her father. She said, "Yes; he heard that you were coming home and wondered if you would not come to see him."

I went to the room where he was lying in bed and found him very ill and very approachable. In fact, his wife was trying to read the Bible to him. I took the Bible and read to him passages that point out our need of a Savior, God's love to us though we are sinners, and God's way of salvation. I then explained the way of salvation and prayed with him.

The next evening, I met his daughter again and asked her if I could see her father again. "Yes; he was hoping that you would come again and wondered if you would not."

I heard that he had been talking about me and about my son, whose acquaintance he had also made. A part of the time, he had been in delirium; and in his delirium, he had been talking about my son. I went to see him and found him perfectly clear in mind, but I felt that he could not pull through the night. I was more definite than the night before as I explained the way of life simply and fully, and he professed to accept Christ. I then knelt by his bed and prayed and afterward asked him to follow me in prayer. Word by word, he repeated me in the confession of his sin, in the expression of his belief in God's testimony about Jesus Christ—that Jesus had borne his sin in His own body on the tree; he asked God to forgive his sins, because Jesus had borne them in His own body on the cross; he told his heavenly Father that he trusted He had forgiven his sins, because of the atoning death of Christ; and then he told his Father that, if it was His will, he wished to be raised from this bed of sickness in order to serve Christ, but that if it was not His will to raise Him up, he was willing to be taken from this world and to depart and be with Christ.

When I arose, he seemed to be resting in the Lord Jesus. Two hours later, there was a rap on my door, and a lady came in and told me that he had passed away, trusting in Christ, about an hour after I had left.

244 Real Salvation

Lay Siege by Letters

There are many whom we cannot reach by a conversation whom we can reach by letters. A letter is sometimes more effective than direct personal conversation. A letter can be read at leisure and apart by oneself, and it can be read again and again. Eternity alone will reveal how many thousands have been won to Christ by the medium of letters from earnest Christians. There is tremendous power in the pen. Have you consecrated your pen to Christ? You may not be able to write books, but you can write letters, and letters are oftentimes more effective than books.

I know an American woman in humble circumstances who makes a practice of writing letters to criminals in prison all over the United States. She has to do extra work to make the money to pay the postage on these letters, but her efforts have been greatly blessed of God. I have personally known a number of criminals in different states who have been won to Christ by the letters of this godly woman.

In one of our missions, one of the most prominent men in the town was just leaving the town as we entered it. In the good providence of God, the steamer upon which he was sailing ran aground, and he had to return to the town. The next day was the Sabbath, and this man attended the meeting and was somewhat impressed. A leading lady of the town, hearing that he had been unable to get away and had been at the meeting, wrote him a letter urging him to accept Christ. This letter was accompanied by much prayer and did its work; he came forward publicly and told the great throng that he had accepted Christ. His conversion made a great impression upon the whole community.

Lay Siege by Tracts, Booklets, and Books

There is great power in well-chosen tracts and books. The writer of one tract, before his death, had letters from sixteen hundred people, saying they had been brought to Christ by that tract. Sometimes, you can hand a tract directly to those you wish to lead out; but, oftentimes, you can reach people more effectively by indirection. They would be offended if you handed them a tract, but if you leave it around, they will pick it up out of curiosity and read it. If there is an especially difficult case, it is well to invite him to your home. On the first night of a person's arrival, retire early; have some well-chosen book that you wish for him to read, make sure that every other book is taken out of his room, and see to it that there is a good light to read by. When he has been shown to his room at this unusually early hour, he will not wish to retire for the night. He will say, "Why do these people go to bed so early? I wonder if there is not something to read." He will look around and find there is just one book in the room to read. He will say, "It is a religious book," and very likely will add, "I don't care for religious books, but there is nothing else to read." He will sit down and begin to read it. All this time, you are in another room, praying for him.

Sometimes, it is well to put a tract under a person's pillow. When he is restless in the night, he feels the touch of that tract as he puts his hand under his pillow. All men are naturally curious; he will find a light and read the tract and may be saved by it.

A young man in London was urged again and again by his godly mother to accept Christ. He was determined that he would not, and at last, to escape the unceasing pleadings of his mother, he left home and went to a town in the north of England. He obtained lodgings in this town. The woman with whom he obtained them was a godly woman. Seeing this young man away from home, her heart went out toward him, and she put a tract under his pillow. When he went to bed that first night, away from home, he was restless; putting his hand under his pillow, he felt the tract and wondered what it was. He turned on a light and found that it was a religious tract. He said to himself, "Here, I have ran away from home to get rid of my mother's constant pleadings with me to become a Christian, and the first night away from home, I find a tract under my pillow; I might as well give in." And he did, and accepted Christ.

A friend of mine was once visiting a godless home. When he left the home, he left his Bible behind him, with a tract inside. After he had gone, the lady of the house opened his Bible, out of curiosity, and it opened to where the tract lay. She read the tract and was converted by it, and when he came back several days after for his Bible, he found that several members of the household had been led to Christ by the tract.

By such methods as this, and by all methods—by every kind of sanctified ingenuity—lay siege to those whom you have selected to win for Christ.

General Suggestions

The following are a few general suggestions as to the spirit in which the work is to be done.

Be Persistent

It is at this point that many would-be soulwinners fail. They make one or two attempts to lead others to Christ, and when they appear to have been unsuccessful, they give it up. No one can win souls to Christ this way. The way to succeed in any kind of business is by persistence. One can do pretty much anything in this world that he makes up his mind to do, if he will only stick to it. Stick-to-itiveness is a priceless grace, especially in soulwinning. If one effort does not succeed, make another; if the second does not succeed, make another; if the hundredth does not succeed, make another. Don't give up until you win, even if it takes fifty years.

I prayed and worked for the salvation of one man for fifteen years. I seemed to be making absolutely no headway. He wandered further and further from God, but I did not give up. There could hardly be a more unlikely case than he, utterly sunken in worldliness and sin; but I won, and I had the joy of seeing that man become a preacher of the gospel. Today, he is in heaven. When he was converted, his old friends could hardly believe it; it seemed to them utterly preposterous that such a person had been converted, but he had. You can win anyone to Christ if you are willing to keep at it.

Be Courteous

There is nothing that costs less, and there are few things that pay better in this world, than courtesy. It pays in business. But there is no place where it pays better than in soulwinning work. You may be poor, but you can be well-bred. Treat every man with whom you deal as a gentleman and every woman with whom you deal as a lady. I have seen people go at others in a most overbearing, discourteous, and irritating way. They assume an air of superiority. They treat the one with whom they are dealing as if he had no sense; they act as if they were determined to pound their ideas into another man's head. Now, every person of sense and character resents this kind of treatment. The person with whom you deal may be utterly wrong, yet you can treat his opinions and his feelings with consideration and kindness. You are far more likely to win him in that way. Never have a heated argument with a person you would lead to Christ. Listen to what he has to say. Treat him with deference. It is quite possible to expose the hatefulness of another's sin in a courteous and considerate way. You will produce far deeper conviction that way.

Also avoid all familiarities with those with whom you are deal-ing. A gentleman or a lady always resents undue familiarity. I have seen a man sit down in our after-meetings beside a young woman and put his arm along the back of her seat. Any lady resents such conduct, and she is likely to get up and leave the meeting. It is all right when, in prayer, a man puts his arm around a drunkard who has not had a kindly action shown him in years. It is all right for a lady to put her arm around a fallen sister who has had nothing but curses and abuse for years. If it is the first touch of a loving hand that she has felt for many a long year, it may soften her heart. But every worker must be careful to treat everyone with whom he deals with all due deference and courtesy.

Be Earnest

Many would-be soulwinners are utterly professional. Those with whom they deal cannot but see that they have no real interest in their spiritual welfare, no deep concern for their souls. Such a worker may have a large technical knowledge of the Bible, and of just the right passages to use in dealing with certain classes of men and women, but his knowledge counts for nothing unless there is deep reality and earnestness to back it up. Other workers may have a comparatively small knowledge of the Word and yet such an ear-nest love for the perishing that their little knowledge is used vastly beyond the superior knowledge of the other.

In a certain town, there was an unbelieving blacksmith. He was well-read in worldly literature and rejoiced in his power to defeat any opponent in argument. A deacon in the town had a great longing for this man's salvation. He read up on the same literature the blacksmith enjoyed and the arguments in reply to it. When he thought he had mastered the subject, he called upon this black-smith to persuade him that he was wrong in his infidel opinions, but he proved no match for the blacksmith. In a few moments, the blacksmith had shattered his arguments and defeated him utterly. The deacon knew that he was right, but he could not prove it to the blacksmith; but in his deep yearning for the salvation of the man, he burst into tears and said, "All I can say is, I have a great spiritual concern for your soul."

Then he left, went to his home, burst in upon his wife, and said, "Wife, I am a botch on God's work. God knows I really love that blacksmith's soul, and I went down to prove to him that he was wrong; but in a few minutes, he beat me utterly in argument. I am only a botch on God's work." He then retired to his room and knelt down to pray. He said, "O God, I am only a botch on Thy work. Thou knowest that I have a real desire for that man's salvation, but I have failed utterly in my attempt. I am only a botch on Thy work."

Soon after he had left the blacksmith's shop, the blacksmith went into his house and said to his wife, who was a godly woman, "Wife, Deacon — was just over talking to me. He used one argument I did not understand. He said he had a great spiritual concern for my soul. What did he mean?"

His wife, who was a canny woman, said, "You had better go and ask him."

The blacksmith hung up his apron and went across the fields to the deacon's house. Just as he ascended the piazza and was at the door, he heard the deacon in prayer, saying that he was a botch on God's work. The blacksmith pushed open the door and cried, "Deacon, you are no botch on God's work. I thought I knew all the arguments for Christianity, and that I could answer them all, but you used an argument this morning I had never heard before and cannot answer. You said you had a great spiritual concern for my soul."

The deacon had the joy, then and there, of leading that man to Christ. Have you a great spiritual concern for the souls of the perishing? If not, the sooner you get it, the better for you and for the lost.

Be Winsome

A winsome manner goes a long way in soulwinning. It is just as easy to smile as it is to scowl. It is just as easy to be genial and winning as it is to be rude and repellant. Some people seem to take pride in their brusque, overbearing manner; but brusqueness is not a fruit of the Spirit. "*The fruit of the Spirit is love, joy, peace, longsuffering, gentleness, goodness, faith, meekness, temperance*" (Galatians 5:22–23). A winning manner, the outcome of a life controlled by the Holy Spirit, is of more importance in soulwinning than a theological education. Acts of kindness go a long way toward paving the way to the gate of a man's heart.

A young missionary visiting Chicago found an unbeliever dying of consumption. Day after day, she visited him with little gifts to make his last days on earth pleasanter. One day, it would be a glass of jelly; another day, something else. After about thirty days of such kindly ministrations, she became fearful that his time was short. She came to me at the close of my Bible class one Sunday afternoon and said, "Won't you come with me to see a dying man? I am afraid he will not live through the night."

I hurried down with her to the poor room where the unbeliever lay dying. His wife was a Roman Catholic. I sat down by his bed and read the Scriptures to him—the Scriptures that make plain the love of God for sinners, the death of Christ in our stead, and the way of salvation through our crucified Savior. I then asked him if I might pray with him, and he consented. I prayed that God would open his eyes to show him that he was a lost sinner, but that Jesus had borne all his sins in His own body upon the cross. Then I began to sing in a low tone by his bed,

> Just as I am, without one plea,
> But that Thy blood was shed for me,
> And that Thou bidst me come to Thee,
> O Lamb of God, I come.[4]

I sang it through, verse after verse, until I reached the last verse; and then I heard the dying infidel, in a feeble voice, join with me in the verse that goes,

> Just as I am, Thou wilt receive,
> Wilt welcome, pardon, cleanse, relieve;
> Because Thy promise I believe,
> O Lamb of God, I come, I come.

I looked up and asked him if he had really come. He said that he had. He passed into eternity that night. I was asked to conduct the funeral services. Standing by his casket, with his unsaved friends standing on the other side, I told how utterly insufficient his infidel views had proven in the time of crisis and of death, and how, in his last hours, he had accepted Christ. Then I said, "Who of you today will take the same step?"

One stalwart unbeliever reached his hand across the casket and said, "I will. I have sympathized with this man in his infidel views, but I give it up now and take Christ." His wife also accepted Christ and is today a devoted member of our church in Chicago. But it was not my brief visit that had won him to Christ. It was the kindly, Christlike conduct of the young woman missionary.

---

4. Charlotte Elliott, "Just as I Am, Without One Plea," 1835.

Be Full of Love

Love is the first fruit of the Spirit, and it is the all-conquering power in soulwinning work. I doubt if there is a heart on earth that cannot be conquered by love. We have in America a devoted Christian woman of culture, refinement, and position, with a heart full of love for the most outcast and abandoned. She has devoted much of her life and strength to getting matrons appointed in jails and lockups for the reception and charge of female prisoners. Oftentimes, she has found it hard work to induce the authorities to put a woman in charge of the female prisoners. In one city, they said to her, "Mrs. Barney, no woman can manage the class of women with whom we have to do."

Mrs. Barney replied, "You never had a prisoner that I could not manage."

"We would like to have you try your hand on 'Old Sal,'" was the laughing reply.

"I would like to," the gentle lady responded.

"Well, the next time we have her under arrest, we will send for you."

Not long after, early one morning, Mrs. Barney received word that "Old Sal" was under arrest, and she hurried down to the lockup. She asked to be shown to her cell.

The sergeant at the desk protested that it was not safe. "Look there," he said to Mrs. Barney, pointing to four policemen with torn clothes and faces. "There is a specimen of Old Sal's handiwork. It took these four men to arrest her."

"Never mind," said Mrs. Barney. "Show me to her cell."

"Well, if you must go, an officer must go with you."

"No, I will go alone. Just let the turnkey open the door, and I will go to her cell alone." Before going down, Mrs. Barney had asked the sergeant at the desk for Old Sal's right name.

"Why," he had said, "we always call her Old Sal."

"Yes," had said Mrs. Barney, "but I wish her right name. What is her right name?"

"It is a long time since we first booked her, and we always book her now as Old Sal."

"Look up her right name," Mrs. Barney had insisted.

The sergeant had gone back through the books and had found Old Sal's proper name.

The turnkey opened the door and pointed to her cell down the corridor. When Mrs. Barney reached the door, she saw a wild creature with torn gray hair, disheveled garments, and glaring eyes crouching in the corner of the cell and waiting to spring upon the first policeman who should enter.

"Good morning, Mrs. —," said Mrs. Barney, calling her by her true name.

"Where did you get that name?" said the poor creature.

Without answering her question, Mrs. Barney said, "Sally, do you remember the first time you were committed here?"

"My God," she cried, "don't I? I spent the whole night crying on the floor of my cell."

"Suppose," said Mrs. Barney, "there had been some kind Christian woman here to have received you that night and to have treated you gently; do you think your life would have been different?"

"Altogether different," she replied.

"Well," said Mrs. Barney, "I am trying to get them to appoint a woman in this lockup to receive young girls when they are brought here for the first time, as you were when you were brought here that first night. Will you help me?"

"I will do all that I can," she said.

All the time, Mrs. Barney had been drawing nearer and was now kneeling by Sally's side upon the cell floor, gathering up her torn and grizzled hair, fastening it up with pins taken out of her own hair, pulling together the torn shreds of her garments, and fastening them with pins taken from her own garments. The work was now done, and Mrs. Barney, rising to her feet, said, "Sally, we are going into the courtroom. If you will be good, they will appoint a woman in this lockup. Shall I go in on your arm, or will you go in on mine?"

The strong woman looked at Mrs. Barney and said, "I think I am stronger than you are. You had better go in on my arm." And in they went into the court, the gentle lady leaning on the arm of the hardened old criminal. Sally restrained herself through the whole trial and answered the judge's questions pleasantly. She forgot to restrain herself once, swearing at the judge, but immediately she begged his pardon. Everybody was amazed at the transformation. A woman was appointed as matron of the jail; but, best of all, Sally got her feet upon the Rock of Ages, and today, Old Sal is in the glory. Love had conquered. It always will.

Oh, men and women, young and old, go out to do this work; seek the filling of the Spirit that God is so ready to give to us all; and in the power of that Spirit, day after day and month after month and year after year, labor on for the definite salvation of the definite souls that God shall bring your way. Our time is drawing near; let us make the most of it.

AFTERWORD:
HOW TO BE SAVED

A Christian is someone who believes in and takes the following steps in order to be saved and have a real relationship and genuine experience with the real God.

The Fundamentals of the Bible

A Christian understands, accepts, and believes the following truths from the Bible:

1. **All men are sinners and fall short of God's perfect standard.** *"For all have sinned, and come short of the glory of God"* (Romans 3:23).

2. **Sin, which is imperfection in our lives, denies us eternal life with God.** But God sent His Son Jesus Christ to die for us, giving us eternal life by believing in Him. Romans 6:23 states, *"For the wages of sin is death; but the gift of God is eternal life through Jesus Christ our Lord."*

3. **You can be saved, and you are saved by faith in Jesus Christ.** You cannot be saved by your good works, because they are not "good enough." But God's good work of sending Jesus Christ to save us, and our response of believing—of having faith—in Jesus Christ is what saves each of us. Ephesians 2:8–9 states, *"For by grace are ye saved through faith; and that not of yourselves: it is the gift of God: not of works, lest any man should boast."*

4. God did not wait for us to become perfect in order to accept or unconditionally love us. **He sent Jesus Christ to save us, even though we are sinners.** So Jesus Christ died to save us from our sins and to save us from eternal separation from God. Romans 5:8 states, *"But God commendeth his love toward us, in that, while we were yet sinners, Christ died for us."*

5. **God loved the world so much that He sent His one and only Son to die, so that we, by believing in Jesus Christ, would obtain eternal life.** John 3:16 states, *"For God so loved the world, that he gave his only begotten Son, that whosoever believeth in him should not perish, but have everlasting life."*

6. **If you believe in Jesus Christ, and in what He did on the cross for us by dying there for us, you know for a fact that you have been given eternal life.** *"These things have I written unto you that believe on the name of the Son of God; that ye may know that ye have eternal life, and that ye may believe on the name of the Son of God"* (1 John 5:13).

7. If you confess your sins to God, you can know for sure that He hears you, and that **His response to you is to forgive you of your sins, so that they are not remembered against you and not attributed to you ever again.** *"If we confess our sins, he is faithful and just to forgive us our sins, and to cleanse us from all unrighteousness"* (1 John 1:9). If you believe these verses, or want to believe these verses, pray the following:

Lord Jesus, I need You. Thank You for dying on the cross for my sins. I open the door of my life and ask You to save me from my sins and to give me eternal life. Thank You for forgiving me of my sins and giving me eternal life. I receive You as my Savior and Lord. Please take control of the throne of my life. Make me the kind of person You want me to be. Help me to understand You, to know You, and to learn how to follow You. Free me from all of the things in my life that prevent me from following You. In the name of the one and only and true Jesus Christ, I ask all these things now, amen.

Does this prayer express your desire to know God and His love? If you are sincere in praying this prayer, Jesus Christ will come into your heart and your life, just as He said he would.

It often takes courage to decide to become a Christian. It is the right decision to make, but it is difficult to fight against the part of ourselves that wants to hang on, or to fight against the part of ourselves that has trouble changing. The good news is that you do not need to change yourself. Just cry out to God and pray, and He will begin to change you. God does not expect you to become perfect before you come to Him—not at all. This is why He sent Jesus, so that we would not have to become perfect before coming to know God.

Steps to Take as a New Christian

Here are some steps to take once you have asked Jesus to come into your life.

1. Read Psalm 23 (in the middle of the Old Testament—the first half of the Bible) and meditate on it.

2. Read Psalm 91 and meditate on it.

3. Read the New Testament books John, Romans, and 1 John, and meditate on them.

4. Tell someone close to you of your prayer and that you are seeking God.

5. Obtain some books by sound theologians and begin to read them, so that you can understand more about God and how He works.

6. Pray—that is, talk to and with God—thanking Him for saving you, telling Him your fears and concerns, and asking Him for help and guidance.

7. Tell someone about the great decision you have made today!

Answers to Common Questions

1. Does the "being saved" process work only for those who believe?

For the person who is not yet saved, his understanding of (1) his state of sin and (2) God's personal love and care for him, as well as His desire and ability to save him, is what enables a person to be saved. So, yes, the "being saved" process works only for those who believe in Jesus Christ alone and place their faith in Him and in His work on the cross.

2. If so, how does belief save a person?

Belief saves a person because of what it allows God to do in his heart and soul. But it is not simply the fact of a belief. The issue is not belief but rather what we believe. If a person believes in salvation by faith alone in Jesus Christ, then that belief saves him. Why? Because he is magical? No, because of the sovereignty of God, and because of what God does in him when he asked Him into his heart and life. When a person decides to place his faith in Jesus Christ, asks Him to forgive his sins, and invites Jesus Christ into his life and heart, this is what saves him.

At the moment when a person sincerely believes and asks God to save him (as described above), God will take the life of that person and, in accordance with His will for him, will take his sins (all sins past, present, and future) and allocate them to the category of "one of those people who accepted the free gift of eternal salvation that God offers."

From that point forward, his sins are no longer counted against him, because his is an account that has been paid by the shed blood of Jesus Christ. And there is no person who could ever sin so much that God's love would not be good enough for him, or that the penalty of death for which Jesus Christ paid the price would somehow not be enough to cover him (otherwise, sin would be more powerful than Jesus Christ, which is not true).

Two Lies That Are Often Believed

Sometimes, people have trouble believing in Jesus Christ because of two lies.

The first lie is that they are *not* sinners. Usually, this means that a person has not committed a "serious" sin, such as murder; but God says that all sins separate us from God, even supposedly "small" sins. We humans tend to categorize sin as "more serious" or "less serious" because we do not understand just how serious "small" sins are. Since we are all sinners, we all need God in order to have eternal salvation.

The second lie is that they are not good enough for Jesus Christ to save them. This lie is believed mostly by those who reject the free offer of salvation through Christ Jesus because they are unwilling to believe. After death, they will believe; but they can choose eternal life only *before* they die. The fact is that no one is good enough for Jesus Christ to save. That is why Paul wrote, *"For all have sinned, and come short of the glory of God"* (Romans 3:23). Thankfully, that is not the end of the story, because he also wrote, *"For the wages of sin is death; but the gift of God is eternal life through Jesus Christ our Lord."* (Romans 6:23).

That free offer of salvation is clarified in the following passage:

> *For God so loved the world, that he gave his only begotten Son, that whosoever believeth in him should **not perish**, but have everlasting life. For God sent not his Son into the world to condemn the world; but that the world **through him** might be saved.* (John 3:16–17)

Prayers That Count

I don't make the rules any more than you do. I just want to help you to know how to reach God and to know that God cares about you personally.

The prayers that make it to heaven, where God dwells, are only those that are prayed directly to Him through Jesus Christ or in the name of Jesus Christ.

God hears our prayers because we obey the methods He has established for us to reach Him. If we want Him to hear us, then we must use the methods that He has given us to communicate with Him.

In the New Testament, He explains what those methods entail: (1) talking (praying) to God in accordance with His will, and (2) coming to Him in the name of Jesus Christ. Here are some examples from the New Testament:

*Then Peter said, Silver and gold have I none; but such as I have give I thee: **In the name of Jesus Christ of Nazareth** rise up and walk.* (Acts 3:6)

*And this did she many days. But Paul, being grieved, turned and said to the spirit, I command thee **in the name of Jesus Christ** to come out of her. And he came out the same hour.* (Acts 16:18)

*But Barnabas took him, and brought him to the apostles, and declared unto them how he had seen the Lord in the way, and that he had spoken to him, and how he had preached boldly at Damascus **in the name of Jesus**."* (Acts 9:27)

*And such trust have we **through Christ** to God-ward [toward God].* (2 Corinthians 3:4)

*Wherefore thou art no more a servant, but a son; and if a son, then an heir of God **through Christ**.* (Galatians 4:7)

*That in the ages to come he might show the exceeding [spiritual] riches of his grace in his kindness toward us **through Christ Jesus**.* (Ephesians 2:7)

*And the peace of God, which passeth all understanding, shall keep your hearts and minds **through Christ Jesus.***

(Philippians 4:7)

*Being grieved that they taught the people, and preached **through Jesus** the resurrection from the dead.*   (Acts 4:2)

*First, I thank my God **through Jesus Christ** for you all, that your faith is spoken of throughout the whole world.*

(Romans 1:8)

*Likewise reckon ye also yourselves to be dead indeed unto sin, but alive unto God **through Jesus Christ** our Lord.*

(Romans 6:11)

*For the wages of sin is death; but the gift of God is **eternal life through Jesus Christ our Lord.***   (Romans 6:23)

*I have therefore whereof I may glory **through Jesus Christ** in those things which pertain to God.*   (Romans 15:17)

*To God only wise, be glory **through Jesus Christ** for ever. Amen.*

(Romans 16:27)

*If any man minister, let him do it as of the ability which God giveth: that God in all things may be glorified **through Jesus Christ**, to whom be praise and dominion for ever and ever. Amen.*   (1 Peter 4:11)

*That the blessing of Abraham might come on the Gentiles **through Jesus Christ**; that we might receive the promise of the [Holy] Spirit through faith.*   (Galatians 3:14)

*Which he shed on us abundantly **through Jesus Christ our Savior.*** (Titus 3:6)

Make you perfect in every good work to do his will, working in you that which is wellpleasing in his sight, through Jesus Christ; to whom be glory for ever and ever. Amen.

(Hebrews 13:21)

⁓

If a person wanted to become a Christian, what would he pray? Something such as the following:

God, I am praying so that You will help me. Please help me to want to know You better. Please help me to become a Christian.

God, I admit that I am not perfect. I understand that You cannot allow anyone into heaven who is not perfect and holy. I understand that if I believe in Jesus Christ and in what He did, You, God, will see my life through the sacrifice of Jesus Christ, and that this will allow me to have eternal life and to know that I am going to heaven.

God, I admit that I have sin and other imperfect things in my life. Please forgive me of my sins. I believe that Jesus Christ is the Son of God, that He came to earth to save those who ask Him, and that He died to pay the penalty for all my sins.

I understand that Jesus physically died and physically arose from the dead, and that You can forgive me because of the death and resurrection of Jesus Christ. I thank You for dying for me and for paying the price for my sins. I believe in You and thank You, Lord God, with all my heart, for Your help and for sending Your Son to die and be raised from the dead.

I pray that You would help me to read Your Word, the Bible. I renounce anything in my life, my thoughts, and my actions that is not from You, and I do this in the name of Jesus Christ. Help me not to be spiritually deceived. Help me to grow, to boldly follow You, and to be a good example to others. Develop within me a love of Your Word, the Bible, and please bring into my life people and situations that will help me to better understand how to live my life as Your servant.

Help me to share the good news with those who are willing to hear it. I ask these things in the name of Jesus Christ, and I thank You again for what You have done for me. Amen.

Please remember, Christianity is *never* forced. No one can force a person to become a Christian. God does *not* recognize any person's desire for Him unless it is genuine and from the inside.

ABOUT THE AUTHOR

Reuben Archer Torrey (1856–1928) was born in Hoboken, New Jersey, on January 28, 1856. He graduated from Yale University in 1875 and from Yale Divinity School in 1878.

Upon his graduation, Dr. Torrey became a Congregational minister. A few years later, he joined Dwight L. Moody in his evangelistic work in Chicago and became the pastor of the Chicago Avenue Church. He was selected by D. L. Moody to become the first dean of the Moody Bible Institute of Chicago. Under his direction, Moody Institute became a pattern for Bible institutes around the world.

Torrey is respected as one of the greatest evangelists of modern times. At the turn of the century, he began his evangelistic tours and crusades. He spent the years of 1903–1905 in a worldwide revival campaign, along with the famous song leader Charles McCallon Alexander. Together, they ministered in many parts of the world and reportedly brought nearly 100,000 souls to Jesus. Torrey continued worldwide crusades for the next fifteen years, eventually reaching Japan and China. During those same years, he served as Dean of the Bible Institute of Los Angeles and pastored the Church of the Open Door in that city.

Torrey longed for more Christian workers to take an active part in bringing the message of salvation through Christ to a lost and dying world. His straightforward style of evangelism has shown thousands of Christian workers how to become effective soulwinners.

Dr. Torrey died on October 26, 1928. He is well remembered today for his inspiring devotional books on the Christian life, which have been translated into many different languages. Woven throughout his many books, the evangelistic message that sent Torrey around the world still ministers to all whose hearts yearn to lead men, women, and children to salvation through Jesus Christ.

Welcome to Our House!
We Have a Special Gift for You ...

It is our privilege and pleasure to share in your love of Christian classics by publishing books that enrich your life and encourage your faith.

To show our appreciation, we invite you to sign up to receive a specially selected **Reader Appreciation Gift**, with our compliments. Just go to the Web address at the bottom of this page.

God bless you as you seek a deeper walk with Him!

WE HAVE A GIFT FOR YOU

whpub.me/classicthx

WHITAKER
HOUSE